T. ATKINS

THE EDGE OF Discontent

DesKor Inc

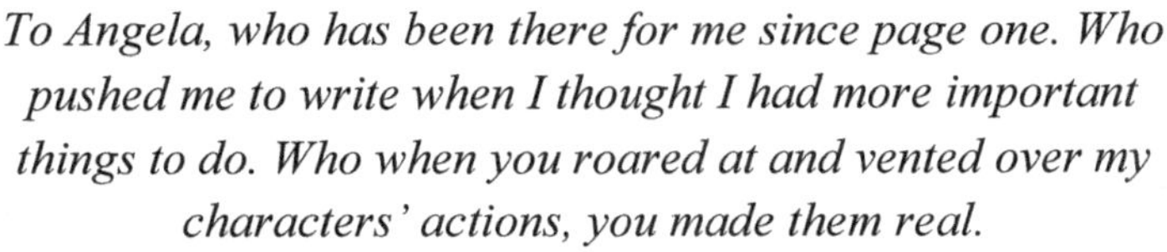

To Angela, who has been there for me since page one. Who pushed me to write when I thought I had more important things to do. Who when you roared at and vented over my characters' actions, you made them real.
Thank you for being the first person who willingly wanted to read anything I ever wrote, and most of all, THANK YOU for being my friend.

CHAPTER 1

THE SOUND OF THE alarm startled Trudy from her sleep. *Traitor*, she thought, reaching over to turn it off.

She sat up, swinging her legs over the side of the bed, waiting for her eyes to adjust to her surroundings, while scanning the room for her pajama bottoms. Her husband, James, worked nights, so the windows were covered with thick drapery to keep the morning light out.

Spying her pajama bottoms, Trudy grabbed them and headed to the bathroom to relieve herself and wash her face so that she could begin her day. First thing, wake the kids— well, one kid. Cori would already be up. Her daughter, perpetually concerned with her appearance, would most likely be in the bathroom getting ready.

Stopping at her son Eric's bedroom door, Trudy could hear the beeping of the alarm clock, along with the sounds of light snoring, as he slept through the alarm.

"Eric," called Trudy, knocking on the door. "Eric."

"Hmmm," came a sound from inside the room.

"Eric, time to get up."

"Okay, Mom," he responded drowsily.

"Eric, seriously, you need to get up."

The sound of rustling sheets could be heard from inside the bedroom as the alarm continued to beckon.

"Get up," she said again, a little louder this time." And turn that alarm off."

There was music coming from inside the bathroom. Trudy tapped lightly on the door.

"Yes, Mom?" Cori answered snappishly, turning down the music.

"Just wanted to check on you."

Cori turned the music back up without answering.

Oh, to be a teenager again. Trudy headed downstairs to prepare breakfast.

Why was growing up even a requirement? As a child, she had dreaded each birthday. Her only wish when she blew out her candles; to stay young forever. Who in their right mind wanted to be a grown-up anyway, only to be stuck in this repetitive routine of getting up at the same time each day, going to work, and coming back home? And doing it all over again, *each and every day.* There had to be more to being an adult than this.

Luckily, today had offered a little change. Her best friend Shawna had asked to meet up after work today. If she could just get James to agree to pick Cori up from school, then Trudy could meet with Shawna as soon as she got off. However, even that was wishful thinking. It was more than likely that Shawna would call and cancel, as she usually did.

The kids eventually made their way downstairs. Tossing their backpacks by the front door and complaining about how unfair life could be—looking forward to the day when they were adults and could do what they wanted and not have to get up early and go to school.

Trudy shook her head and laughed to herself. *If they only knew.*

They each took a seat at the kitchen island, strangely without any complaints about the breakfast Trudy had laid out for them. Today would be cereal and milk. She had not felt like cooking this morning.

Eric, a mixture of her and James, was four years younger than Cori and now a few inches taller than her. Thanks to a growth spurt at the beginning of the year. Before, he had been short and stubby and constantly picked on by his sister. Now tall and lanky, he still gave Cori plenty of reasons to taunt him.

Cori, dark-haired, with slanted brown eyes and a pugged nose, was a younger version of her mother, but would vehemently deny it when anyone pointed it out. "No," she would say. I look like my dad."

"Ow, Cori," Eric exclaimed.

"What happened?" asked Trudy, coming out of the kitchen pantry.

"Cori just stuck me with a pin or something."

"What are you talking about?" asked Cori, appearing incredulous to the accusation.

"Cori, seriously. Can't we go one morning without you harassing your brother?"

Just as Cori was about to either explain or continue to deny the accusations, Trudy heard the loud roar of an engine that could only be the kid's school bus coming up the street. She quickly hustled the kids out of the door, making sure they both had everything. Whatever Cori had to say would have to be left for another time.

As she watched the kids board the bus, Trudy was

overcome by a feeling of nostalgia.

This was her son's first year in high school and her daughter's last, and Trudy wasn't sure how she felt about Cori leaving home for college next year. Although she loved her daughter, the two of them had never been close. She thought it had a lot to do with her upbringing. Trudy's family had never been big on love. They didn't hug and say I love you to one another, and by the time Trudy figured out that things like affection were necessary, it had seemed too late to rectify the problem with her kids.

Despite not being ready to see Cori off to college, Trudy was glad it was her last year of high school. Maybe then, she would get over her need to fit in. Cori had her own group of friends, but for some reason, she still constantly worried about what others thought of her. Cori didn't just spend a substantial amount of time getting ready for school, but for everywhere they went. Unfortunately, caring about her appearance was not the only side-effect of her need for acceptance; Cori had to have the latest gadgets and name-brand clothes. And it was hard to keep Cori in the latest fashion on one and a half incomes.

James worked for his family, and the air conditioning company hadn't done so well in recent years. Depending on what kind of revenue they brought in for the month, determined whether or not James got paid. This had led to countless arguments, which led to nowhere. James felt like he owed his family and would not budge on seeking outside employment, not even a part-time job. He felt that a part-time job would take away time that could be better spent with his family. Trudy guessed that the bed must be his family, because that seemed to be the only place that occupied his time when he wasn't at work.

It wouldn't be long before James came home, and Trudy needed to get ready for her job at the hardware store, where she was in charge of the payroll and company invoices. But first, she had to walk the dog.

Trudy opened up the cage door, offering escape to their 8-year-old boxer Blue. When she released the latch, he lifted his head, barely acknowledging her. After a few taps on the cage, he finally exited, stretching as he headed towards the door.

Trudy could blame the prolonged morning ritual on his age, but she could not remember a time when it hadn't taken him this long to get ready for his morning walk. She placed his harness around him, and they headed out the door.

James was just pulling into the driveway. Immediately upon seeing the car, Blue became excited and began pulling on the leash, trying to get to him. Although this was a common occurrence, Trudy often wondered why he reacted this way. She was the only one who cared for Blue. After the novelty of owning a puppy wore off, both James and the kids lost interest. The only attention Blue got from James was the one time he took the dog out before she got home from work, quickly placing the dog back in the cage afterward.

James got out of the car, ignoring Blue, and he and Trudy exchanged pleasantries as they passed each other in the driveway. An impartial observer would have thought them to be two strangers passing on the street.

Trudy and Blue's walk started as it always did. He relieved himself once in the yard, and then they turned left, walking toward the end of the neighborhood.

"Okay, Blue. So far, so good. It's just you and me today," Trudy cautioned.

Trudy was always a bit anxious on their morning walks.

Blue was very inquisitive and would not listen to commands when people were around, especially people with pets. While Trudy struggled with the leash and shouted, he would strain towards the other dog walker, hoping to get petted or an opportunity to play with the other dog.

As with most mornings, the neighborhood was quiet. The kids were already off to school, and most of the adults had left for work. She and James had purchased their first home in this neighborhood fourteen years ago, tired of paying rent and looking for a place to call their own. The mortgage payments had been a little above their budget, but at the time, it didn't seem to matter. Trudy had fallen in love with the house and the neighborhood as soon as they had driven by.

Though she still loved her home, those mortgage payments that had not seemed to matter at the time, had begun to be a source of frustration. With her now being the primary provider, she worried about making the payment every month. It was starting to look as if she may have to get a second job.

An unexpected jerk to the leash brought Trudy out of her reverie. A neighbor she had never seen before was walking his dog and was about to pass on the opposite side of the street. Trudy shortened the leash and grabbed hold of the harness, digging in her heels.

The man, appearing oblivious to Trudy's plight, slowed down and started to cross the street, now heading towards them. Seeing this, Trudy gritted her teeth and started dragging Blue up the sidewalk in the opposite direction.

Seeming to have gotten the hint, the man reversed directions and continued on his original course, a perplexed look on his face.

After reaching a safe distance where Blue was no longer

looking for the unwelcome parties, unwelcome at least to Trudy, he quickly finished his morning ritual, and they both headed home with Trudy keeping a lookout for any more distractions.

"One adventure down for the day," exclaimed Trudy as she reentered the house. Now, to see if James was still up.

She stepped into the bedroom, her brow furrowing at the sight of her husband, lying across the bed in his soiled work clothes, watching recaps of sports from the previous night. She resisted the urge to complain, knowing she needed a favor from him.

"How was work last night?" asked Trudy, keeping her voice light.

"Same ole, same ole," answered James, barely looking up.

"I was wondering," Trudy sat down on the bed beside him. "If you could pick Cori up from school this afternoon. Shawna wants to meet me after work to hang out for a while, and Cori has to stay over for debate."

"Seems like that girl needs her own car."

Trudy held back the biting remark that was on the tip of her tongue. A car? Where would the money for a car come from? They were barely making the mortgage payments, and Cori had so many extracurricular activities, she didn't have time for a job.

"Yeah, well, that's not going to happen any time soon. Can you pick her up or not?" She didn't know why James couldn't answer a simple question.

"Probably not. I have to go in early."

"Are…you…serious?" asked Trudy, jumping up from the bed, no longer able to hide her frustrations. "You are barely getting paid for the hours you already work, and now you are working overtime?"

"See, this is why I never—"

"You know what," said Trudy, cutting him off before he could finish. "I'll figure out something on my own. I always do." She stormed off into the bathroom, slamming the door behind her.

Trudy pulled into a parking space outside of Dalsin's & Son, a small hardware store, and the employer of her and twenty other employees. As she put the car in park, a small weight seemed to lift off her shoulders. She loved her job. There always seemed to be something calming about working with numbers. To others, it could be a headache trying to make one plus one equal two, but for her, it was simple.

Not simple in a way that meant easy, but honest and unpretentious. It was one of the only things that made sense in her life, the one thing she didn't need to ponder over, like what had happened to her marriage. What happened to the late-night cuddles, the shared laughter over past events that had not seemed so funny at the time? Or why the two kids that used to adore everything about her, now only knew she existed when they needed money?

Yes, numbers had been the only constant in her life, a grounding tool.

The hardware store stood by itself on its own lot with no adjoining businesses. The only nearby buildings were a bank and a gas station, on opposite sides within walking distance.

Though it was common for most people to frequent the big retailers when looking for housewares and fixtures, the hardware store, after being in business for over forty years, was still holding its own.

Trudy made her way into the store, passing a woman carrying an assortment of small plants. She nodded at the woman, who smiled back.

The little bell over the entry door alerted Jennifer, the cashier, to her presence. Jennifer said hello and quickly returned to her phone call, after seeing it was only Trudy.

Keys were everywhere, hanging from endcaps and inside plastic see-thru cases on top of the U-shaped checkout counter. Because the hardware store offered duplicate keys for home and auto, the store's owner made sure they were always in supply.

The rest of the counter held items like sunglasses, hats, and hand-held gardening tools. Bags of potting soil and fertilizer lay on top of pallets on the floor. Red rectangular signs dangled from the ceiling, each one listing about four or five items that could be found on each aisle.

Heading down the center aisle, Trudy made her way to her office at the back of the store. It wasn't very big, but it didn't need to be. She was only there for a few hours a day, and because most of the work she did was on the computer, she only needed her desktop, a small filing cabinet, a desk, and a comfy chair.

Thankfully, the office was far enough away from any noise that could be a distraction. Inside, the lower half of the walls were layered with rustic gray bricks, the same as those used on the outside of the building. The upper half was glass, allowing Trudy to see anyone who passed by. The door, which she rarely closed, was made of glass as well. On the desk were pictures of her family and a cup containing a few pens for making notes.

Trudy sat down, placed her purse under the desk, and powered on the computer. As she waited, she leaned back and contemplated her morning. She wondered if the distance between her and James, or even her children, would always be there. She knew that teenagers could be a bit self-centered at this phase in their lives, but she hoped that things could change.

She wanted to have the family dinners she never had growing up. Before he died, her father had been a long-distance truck driver who was rarely home, and her mother, well that was a story for another day. Trudy wanted things to be different. She wanted a close-knit family, that sat around the kitchen table and had discussions about their day; only problem was, the kids always seemed to have something more important to do.

And then there was James. Things were good with them at one time. Heck, she would have even called them great. There was a time they couldn't keep their hands off each other. Nowadays, there was always some excuse.

Trudy remembered the day they closed on their home.

She, James, and the kids had driven over to the new house with a few of their belongings. When she had gone to the trunk to bring some of their things in, she had been suddenly swept off her feet by James, who insisted he carry her across the threshold. Cori and Eric were already standing by the front door, sheepishly grinning. She found out later that the three of them had planned the whole thing earlier.

"I hope that look on your face means we met our goals this month?"

Trudy looked up to see the store owner standing on the other side of her desk, holding a green folder. Mr. Dalsin was in his early sixties and sported a head of silver-gray hair. Although he never hesitated to lend a helping hand when needed, he still came to work each day in a dress shirt and slacks. Today he had opted for a jacket as well. She had not even heard him come in.

"I was hesitant to disturb you. You seemed to be miles away, and I haven't seen you smile in months."

"Oh no," answered Trudy. "You could never be a disturbance. This is your company, after all. I was only thinking of the day we first moved into our home."

"Oh, yes, yes, I often find myself, especially now in my old age…." Mr. Dalsin lifted his hand to wave Trudy off as she opened her mouth to protest. "Especially now in my old age, I often find myself reflecting on my past. Luckily, I have so much to be grateful for."

"I know you don't want to hear it, but you are not old, and…in answer to your question," Trudy added. "I haven't started work yet, but last time I checked, the company was well on its way to surpassing this month's goals."

"That wasn't the only reason why I stopped by. Do you remember a fella by the name of Matthew Kelly?"

Trudy racked her brain, trying to place the name. She was sure she should know it.

"Matt Kelly," Mr. Dalsin said, placing emphasis on the name. "He left here about five years ago to start his own business. He was my Assistant Manager at the time."

Ah, yes, Matt, she remembered now. She had only been working there a few months before he left. There had been a big going away party for him on his last day.

"Yes, of course, I remember Matt."

"He's in town this week and is stopping by to say hi. I only mentioned it because he asked about you."

Trudy now knew the reason for the suit jacket today. He and Matt must be going out for a business lunch. Most days, Mr. Dalsin ate a lunch prepared by his wife in his office.

Making the added layer unnecessary.

"Why would he ask about me?" Trudy's brow furrowed. "I had just started working here right before he left. We barely said two words to each other, unless it was about work?"

"At first, I wondered the same thing, and then I thought, you must have made an impression. You know you do that, don't you?" Mr. Dalsin gave Trudy a small wink.

"I'll take you at your word," Trudy shook her head self-consciously.

"I know you don't like it when I give you compliments, even though everything I've ever said was true." Seeing that she was about to object, he quickly changed the subject. "I won't bend your ear anymore. I'll let you get back to work. And before I forget. You might be needing this," he said, handing her the folder.

As Mr. Dalsin headed out of the office, he was greeted by a recent new hire, a young man who had been having trouble figuring out how they stored items. He was gripping an inventory list so tightly it had begun to wad in his hands. Trudy wondered how long before Mr. Dalsin would be divested of his suit jacket.

Turning to the computer, she typed in her password and was instantly greeted with a background screen of an old family photo. It was a picture she had taken of her husband and kids on their last family vacation. Both the kids were in middle school then.

She clicked on the folder containing the ledger for this month's expenses and began entering profits, fees, and other costs accrued for the month. Most of the information needed could be found on her computer, linked to a system that kept a record of every purchase or return made at the cash register.

The rest could be found in the folder that Mr. Dalsin handed her before leaving the office.

As Trudy clicked away at the keypad, a tightness in her shoulders began to settle in, and her comfy chair had started to become not so comfortable. A reminder that she had been sitting at the desk for a while without any breaks. Often, she became so engrossed in her work that she forgot the time.

Getting up to stretch, she heard voices coming toward her office. She instinctively knew that it was Matthew Kelly and Mr. Dalsin.

As the voices grew louder, Trudy suddenly became anxious, reaching down to straighten her clothes, making sure her blouse was still tucked into the waistband of her slacks.

Why does it matter how I look?

Matt would be in the office for a few minutes and then off again to parts unknown. He probably didn't even remember what she looked like.

"It matters because you care," Trudy said aloud. Maybe she should check to see if any guck had formed in the corners of her eyes.

Too late, the two men were already entering the office. Matt stood about six inches taller than Mr. Dalsin. Though both men wore suits, Matt's fit as if it had been tailored to him and not selected off the rack. His head was clean-shaven, and the hairs on his face were trimmed into a goatee, accentuating his square jawline.

He was not the man who had left here four years ago.

That man was full of excitement and dreams of making it big. Simply just by the way he held himself, Trudy could tell that this man had obtained those dreams and was full of self-assurance. Success certainly suited him, and he looked as if he knew it.

"Trudy," said Mr. Dalsin. "You remember Matt?"

"Of course." Trudy walked from behind her desk to greet him. "How could I forget?"

"Wow, Trudy, you haven't changed a bit," Matt reached out to grab her hands.

"Neither have you…," Trudy stopped to correct herself when she saw him lift an eyebrow in reaction to her comment. Well, obviously, he had changed; it was the first thing she noticed about him.

"I mean, you have changed," she said, laughing nervously, pulling her hands away. "You know that..."

She stopped, embarrassed with herself. What was wrong with her? This was not like her. You would have thought she had never met an attractive man in her life. And besides, she already knew Matt. They had worked together years ago.

"So," said Mr. Dalsin, appearing a bit uncomfortable himself. "We only stopped by to say hello. Now, we'll let you get back to your work."

Glad they were leaving so she could go back to acting normal, Trudy started back towards her desk when she heard Matt say, "Hope to see you later."

"Um… okay?" responded Trudy.

Matt tapped his fingers against the doorframe and left.

Had it been that long since a man had shown her any attention, that she didn't know how to act? Still feeling embarrassed, Trudy knew she would never be able to concentrate. Maybe calling Shawna would help her by hashing out her reaction so that she could get her mind back on work.

She picked up the phone on her desk and dialed her friend's home number, hoping that she and not her husband would be the one to answer.

"Hey, girl," answered Shawna. "What ya doing calling me in the middle of the day?"

"Is this a good time? I know Greg doesn't like me calling now that he's decided I seemed sneaky, after the last time I came by to visit."

"No. It's fine. You know how he gets. He's gone for his two-week annual deployment."

"Okay, good. I mean, not good for you that your husband's gone," Trudy stammered. "But good—"

"Girl, please. I know what you mean. So, what's going on and why you stumbling all over yourself?"

"Oh, it's nothing. Just sitting here at the office, acting like a fool. A guy that used to work here a few years ago came back for a visit, and I couldn't even put two words together."

"What'd he do, smile at you or something?"

"What's that supposed to mean?" asked Trudy.

"You know what that means. When was the last time James kissed you hello, or even looked in your direction?"

"Well, regardless of that, I am still a married woman. The way I acted, you would have thought I'd been stranded on a deserted island for the last ten years."

"You may not have been on a desert, but I am sure parts of you are probably dry as one," said Shawna, laughing at her own joke.

Trudy rolled her eyes. "I said a deserted island, not the desert. Anyways, are you still meeting me for drinks after work? I have to figure out how to get Cori from school and still meet you at a decent time."

"You know I'm right," said Shawna, not so willing to change the subject as Trudy was. "Just swing by here and pick me up. I'll ride with you to pick up Cori instead of spending money at a restaurant. That way, I won't have to explain to Greg where the money went when he comes back."

In another life, Trudy would have offered to pay for them both, but she could barely afford to treat herself. Picking Shawna up on the way to get Cori would work out great. She could still spend time with her friend and not waste money on things she could barely afford to.

"You know, that would be better. You haven't seen Cori in a while, and she seems to open up when she's around you."

"What are friends for?" Shawna gave a small laugh.

"Got to go. This work isn't going to do itself."

The phone call hadn't helped. Not only had talking to Shawna not taken her mind off her earlier behavior, Trudy was now starting to question the reason behind it. Why *had* she acted so giddy around Matt?

She also hadn't had anything to eat today, and her stomach had decided, that now was a good time to remind her of it. The constant churning was making her nauseous. She needed to eat something soon.

Her change of plans had freed up a bit of unexpected money, and she could actually go out and get a decent salad from a nearby restaurant. But she knew the money could serve some other useful purpose; there was always some fortuitous expense appearing out of nowhere. Instead, she would walk across the street to the convenience store and see if they had any nutritious options.

She grabbed her cell phone and headed out of her office, stopping to scan the hallway, hoping Matt had already left. She did not want to run into him or Mr. Dalsin. He may want to discuss the awkward exchange that occurred earlier.

Fortunately, the hallway was clear, and she hurried out of her office, hoping her luck would hold. When she entered the hardware store, she saw that it was a lot busier than it had been when she first came in to work. She saw Mr. Dalsin helping a patron, and Matt was nowhere in sight. Jennifer was ringing up a customer, and Trudy stopped to get her attention to let her know, she was just going across the street in case anyone looked for her while she was gone.

As soon as she stepped out of the door, she was immediately aware of the temperature. It had grown warmer while she had been toiling away at her desk. Although the blouse Trudy wore was made from a light material, she knew she would be a bit clammy by the time she made her trip back. But, what was life without a bit of sacrifice, right? Besides, she didn't think anyone would be getting close enough to sniff her out anyway, one of the luxuries of her job.

She made it to the store without any complications and welcomed the cool air when she stepped inside. The store was huge compared to most convenience stores' standards. There was a hotdog bar, a nacho bar, and even a coffee station. There was plenty to choose from for someone on a mediocre budget, but not much if one was trying to stay healthy. Trudy opted for a pack of peanut butter crackers and a bottle of water. Something, she realized after handing the cashier her money, could have been obtained from the vending machine in the hardware store's breakroom, and the water would have been free.

Standing at the register, she saw an assortment of publications. Most of them were about some celebrity and the trouble they were going through. Trudy figured that most of the stories were made up to sell magazines. She wondered if Matt had made it big enough to have stories written about him.

She received her change from the cashier and hurried back

to her office to see if she could find anything about him online.

Sitting back at her desk, she began to question whether researching information about another man was a good idea. What did she hope to find? What kind of revenue did his company earn? Was he dating anyone? Was he married with kids? She had not noticed a ring when he grabbed her hands

earlier, and even if he had been wearing one, how was any of this her business? But then again, what would be the harm in looking up information on an old friend?

She probably wouldn't be able to find out much at work anyway. The computers were set up so they would only allow employees limited access to the internet, in hopes of deterring them from spending too much time browsing when they should be working.

Trudy opened the web browser and typed Matthew Kelly into the search box. She racked her memory, trying to recall what state his company was based in, to narrow down her search. She believed there had been some mention of Houston. The first result brought up an article about joining Matthew Kelly at a Passion and Purpose Live Event in Houston, TX. The second result, Matthew Kelly-Kelly Distribution.

She clicked on the second link. The webpage opened, featuring the company's name and logo in the top left-hand corner with clickable links to the Home, Recent News, and Contact information on the right. In the center of the page was a picture of the man who had stood in her office about twenty minutes ago. Above the photo was his name, Matthew Kelly, CEO. Next to his picture was a short biographical paragraph. It mentioned the degrees he had obtained, when the business was started, and his visions for the company's future, but no mention of any significant other.

Trudy did further research and saw that the company surpassed its projected earnings in its last quarterly report. The business appeared to be doing well. She wondered what Matt's reasons for coming back here were. Mr. Dalsin only mentioned that it was for a visit, but she doubted he would travel back just for a social call. Whatever it was, she was sure it had nothing to do with her.

Now that her pack of crackers had been consumed, she needed to get back to work, if she was going to pick up Shawna and get to the school on time to pick up Cori. The last thing she wanted to hear was her daughter complaining about how many of her other classmates had gone home before she did.

Trudy closed out the browser and opened back up the Excel sheet she'd been working on before she'd been interrupted.

When Trudy pulled in front of Shawna's house, she was already walking out the door. One thing she could say for her friend, she was always punctual, one of the few things they had in common. They also had similar upbringings. Both brought up in families where there was never any talk of love and where discipline was easily chosen over hugs. Probably one of the reasons they had been attracted to the men in their lives.

Shawna's husband had been a sergeant in the military before he retired and treated her more like a soldier than a wife. Even though they had no children, Shawna stayed at home and did not work. Trudy believed that Greg liked it this way so that he could have control over any outside influences that would tempt Shawna into leaving him. The reason she believed Greg had started telling Shawna that Trudy seemed sneaky, and he didn't trust her. She knew, eventually, he would try to find a way to limit their access to each other.

Shawna walked to the car, looking as though she had stepped off the pages of a magazine cover. For someone who was only taking a car trip with her friend to pick up her daughter, she had taken particular care of her appearance. Shawna was wearing makeup, her hair looked to be recently styled, and the outfit she was wearing was more suited for an evening out.

Trudy suddenly became very conscious of how she must look in comparison, and was reminded that she probably didn't smell that great either, after her little trek to the convenience store earlier. She snuck in a quick sniff of her armpits, they seemed okay, but she would have to remind herself to bring a change of clothes to work until the warm weather ended.

Shawna got in the car, a wide smile indicating she was happy to see her.

"What are you all dressed up for?" asked Trudy.

"What this?" Shawna glanced down at herself. "This is how I always dress."

"Yeah, right. I thought drinks were off the table?"

"They still are. I just haven't had a reason to dress up lately and wanted to do something nice for myself. Just because we aren't going out, doesn't mean I can't look good."

That was understandable. It wouldn't hurt if she started putting herself first for once.

During the car ride to school, Shawna chatted away about all the freedom she would have for the next two weeks now that Greg was gone. Thankful that she would not have him around constantly breathing down her neck and monitoring her phone calls.

It's like I can finally breathe," Shawna said, spreading her hands out in front of her. "And talk to you without him always thinking you're trying to put ideas in my head." The usual worry lines that Trudy often noticed on Shawna's forehead were now gone.

Their friendship had lasted more than twenty years, and over the course of that time, Trudy often wondered why Shawna stayed with a man who was so controlling but had been too afraid to ask. Fearful that she would lose her friend if she pushed too hard.

Trudy turned down the road leading to the pick-up line in front of the school and silently cursed herself for not leaving ten minutes earlier. At least twenty cars were in front of her, and she knew Cori would be furious once she reached the front of the line.

Shawna must have been able to read her face. "Guess we should have left sooner, huh?"

"Yeah, I forgot. It's been a while since I had to pick her up."

"Hopefully, she won't bite your head off when she sees me sitting in the car," said Shawna, trying to sound reassuring.

"Yeah, hopefully," Trudy responded with little confidence. "I don't know where that girl gets her attitude from. You would think by the way she acts sometimes, that she has had the worst childhood ever."

"Maybe," said Shawna, playing devil's advocate.

"She's stressed out about school, and you are the easiest person to take it out on."

"I suppose it's possible, but how would I know? She never talks to me."

"Or maybe… she senses things aren't right at home."

Trudy knew it wouldn't take Shawna long to bring up her marriage.

"Even if that were true, she's not treating her father the same way."

"Well, she has always been…Daddy's little girl," Shawna replied.

It was true. When Cori was younger, she and James had been so close that whenever James left the house, she was always right behind him. Usually, when they returned, Cori's face would be sticky from the ice cream she'd been eating, laughing furtively, believing no one was in on their little secret. Trudy had found herself a little jealous of their relationship, wishing she had been as close to her father growing up. She had attempted to form a similar bond with Eric, but he didn't seem to require a close parental relationship like Cori did. Although, sometimes, when he was younger, when she turned over in her sleep, she had often found him curled up beside her.

"Not so much these days," said Trudy. "He doesn't seem to have time for anyone."

Shawna, never being the one to bite her tongue, looked at her friend and asked, "You ever considered that he may be cheating?"

Trudy took a beat before answering. "To be honest, no. I think he's just complacent. He's got the American dream. A house, the wife, two kids, and a dog. I have come to believe that he's just the type of person who's in love with the concept of being married. You know, one of those people who, when you ask about them, are always quick to show you a picture of their family."

Shawna nodded her head, seemingly satisfied with Trudy's answer. "Ever tried shaking things up a bit?"

Trudy moved forward, filling the gap made by the car ahead of her before turning to look at her friend. "Shake things up? I'm done trying. He's always too tired."

"That's not what I meant. You said you think he's the type that's in love with being married. I bet if he thought there was a threat to his marriage, he would start noticing you again."

"You know something I don't know?" asked Trudy, eyeing her friend warily.

"I'm just saying. It doesn't have to be real. You could make something up. What's that guy's name who came into the office today?"

"Who, Matthew?"

"Yeah, you could tell James that he came to town to visit *you*."

"But that's not true." Trudy contradicted her.

"Hmm, he doesn't have to know *that*," Shawna said, raising one eyebrow as she cocked her head to the side.

Trudy was about to tell her friend how crazy she sounded, when she realized she was now in front of the school, and her daughter was staring daggers at her. It wasn't going to be a pleasant ride home.

Fortunately, Cori's mood seemed to shift when she saw Shawna sitting in the front seat, but not by much.

Cori got in the car, tossing her books in the empty seat beside her, and slamming the door. "Umm… you're late."

"I know, honey," said Trudy. "I got here as soon as I could."

Trudy knew it was a lie, but the truth would not have helped to earn her any brownie points with her daughter.

"Excuse me. What, am I invisible?" asked Shawna.

"I'm sorry," said Cori. "But I hate being at school longer than I have to be. Plus, one of my friends invited me over, and I need to get home to shower and change before she comes by to pick me up."

"Oh, really?" Trudy asked. "When were you going to ask me about hanging out, and who is this friend?"

"God, Mom, I'm asking you now, and it's Tara."

"You are not asking me now. You're telling—"

Shawna tapped Trudy on the shoulder, shaking her head with a look that said *Let It Go*.

"Do I have to run everything by you? I'm practically eighteen, an adult."

Trudy bit her tongue, willing herself not to reply. She decided it would be best if she changed the subject. Besides, Tara was a good kid. She got good grades and, unlike her daughter, was always respectful.

"So, what was the debate about?" asked Trudy.

"What?" asked Cori, clearly thrown by the question.

"You stayed over for debate. What was it about?"

"Oh…it was about whether or not to allow cell phones in the classroom."

"Were you for or against?" asked Trudy, trying not to appear too excited that she and her daughter were actually holding a conversation, that would not eventually lead to an argument. Hopefully.

"We actually had to debate both sides, so I'm not sure which one I'm for."

Trudy thought that sounded like the perfect answer for her daughter, who was so easily persuaded by other's opinions.

"So, how're your other classes going? I know the last time we talked, you were making straight A's. Is that still the case?" Shawna asked.

"Of course, you know me," said Cori jokingly.

"What've you been up to, Shawna? I can see you've been shopping lately."

With the conversation turning to both of their favorite subject, the two of them spent the rest of the car ride discussing the latest styles and make-up tips.

When Trudy pulled in front of the house, Cori opened the door before the car even stopped. She got out, waving goodbye to Shawna.

Trudy was a little hurt that she had not been acknowledged in the exchange but scolded herself, knowing that she lived with Cori and saw her every day. It was just that her daughter never said hi, bye, or she would even accept *Your hair is on fire!*

She wished she had something in common with her like Shawna did, but couldn't remember the last time she bought anything new for herself. And whenever she took Cori shopping, she never seemed to like anything Trudy picked out for her. Her response, always an eyeroll followed by a, *Really, Mom?*

Again, Shawna read her face: "Girl, she's a teenager. Don't let it get to you."

"I know you're right, but it hurts when your kids start pulling away from you, and you don't even have the love of your husband to fall back on."

Shawna regarded her with intent, then smiled. "But you know you always have me. I love you."

Trudy nodded, holding back tears that threatened their way out. She knew her friend loved her, and she loved her too, but how much longer would she have Shawna in her life? She knew it wouldn't be long before Greg put an end to their friendship.

CHAPTER 2

TRUDY SAT AT HER laptop, scrutinizing her checking account balance and the monthly bills stacked in front of her, trying to figure out how she was going to pay all of them.

She was sitting in the mudroom she had turned into a small office, after her kids had grown big enough to stop tracking mud into the house. Although the space was a little cramped, she loved it anyway. The clear glass in the side door provided her with enough light to see, and gave her a small view of the outdoors.

The room was decorated with a few paintings of abstract art that she had found at a nearby thrift store. Trudy had also been lucky enough to find a beige, abstract area rug with splashes of navy and red to match the rest of her decor. Her most prized possession was the refinished white oak desk where she currently sat. She had found it at a yard sale and paid for it before considering how heavy it was, or if it would even fit into the small room.

The couple hosting the yard sale had been nice enough to hold onto it for her, until James had been able to get one of the company's trucks, and brought it home with the help of one of his employees.

Today was one of her half-days. She only had payroll, which would only take her a few hours to complete. But as much as she loved her home office, she would much rather be at work right now. At work, when she finished adding up the numbers after paying off any invoices, there was enough money left over because the hardware store always earned a profit. Here, she was trying to figure out if there would be enough money to pay bills and still buy food.

Better yet, if she had it her way, she would still be in high school, where the only things she had to worry about were turning in assignments and figuring out what college she wanted to go to.

Not sitting here having to determine which bills were a priority and which ones she could call and ask for an extension on. She noticed that there had not been any recent deposits into the checking account from James's end, and knew she would again have to have that exhausting conversation about whether or not, he would see a paycheck anytime soon.

Trudy guessed that since she had her laptop opened, she might as well look into updating her resumé. Having a few hours to herself in the mornings may soon be a thing of the past. She felt a brush against her leg and looked down to see Blue pushing past her so that he could curl up on the rug beneath her desk.

She reached down to pet him. "Looks like things may be about to change for the both of us."

Not only would she be giving up her half-days, but it also meant that Blue would be spending more time caged up.

Trudy wasn't sure if she could do that to him. She clicked the X on the document, closing it out. She would hold off looking for another job for a little while longer. Maybe, by the end of the day, James would have some good news for her. If not, she could always borrow a little money from Eric's college fund, though she hoped it wouldn't come to that.

Trudy paid a few of the bills and headed upstairs to see if James was awake. She could hear the sound of light snoring when she opened the door. She went to wake him but thought better of it, knowing how closed off he could be when he was in a *good mood*. She would never get anything out of him if she were to rouse him from his sleep.

She pulled out her cell phone to use the flashlight and grabbed the clothes she had laid out the night before. She'd just send him a text from the office later.

When Trudy entered her office, a visitor was sitting at her desk waiting to greet her. Matt was leaning back in her chair, scrolling through his phone. He immediately stood up when he saw her.

"You're finally here."

"I'm sorry," said Trudy, "Did we have a meeting that I forgot about?"

"No, no." Matt moved from behind her desk, walking towards her. "I just assumed. You were here earlier yesterday. Just figured you'd be here at the same time today."

"Today, I do payroll, so I come in a little later. But you still didn't answer my question. Did we have some sort of meeting I didn't know about?" Trudy asked, sounding agitated.

"Nothing like that. I just thought we could catch up over lunch. I saw you running across the street yesterday with some crackers and a bottle of water, and just figured you might like a change of pace."

Trudy tried her best not to show how mortified she was. She was often told that her emotions showed readily on her face. She'd thought Matt had already left, and she had prided herself on avoiding him.

"I don't usually eat lunch from the convenience store. I just needed to clear my head, and sometimes walking helps."

"Clear your head. Hope that had nothing to do with me?"

The cocky smile on his face belied his comment. Trudy could tell that he hoped it had everything to do with him.

What was going on here? Why had he been asking Mr. Dalsin about her, and why was he waiting for her in her office today? She would have thought he had more pressing matters to attend to while he was in town.

"No, nothing to do with you." Trudy lied. "Did you still have business here with Mr. Dalsin?"

Still looking unconvinced that her little walk across the street had nothing to do with him, Matt seemed to contemplate a response but then shook his head. "No, I have no more business with Mr. Dalsin."

So, it wasn't just a friendly visit.

Deciding it wasn't any of her concern, she returned to his earlier comment. "I just got in the office. I don't think it would be appropriate if I left just after getting here."

"How long does it take you to do payroll?"

"Not long."

"And do you usually come in, do payroll, and then just take back off?

"No," answered Trudy, wondering where this was going.

"So, what's one day? What do you think will happen if you do something out of character for one day?"

"I don't know," said Trudy, smiling. "Maybe time will stop. Anyways, none of that matters. I still have—"

Matt reached out, grabbing her hand, the same as he did yesterday, but this time it was a bit more intimate. Trudy felt goosebumps begin to rise along her arm and neck. She quickly drew her hand away, glancing around her office nervously, trying to remember what she had been saying.

Matt didn't seem bothered by her reaction. In fact, he seemed to be enjoying it. "You're beautiful when you smile."

Trudy felt her cheeks growing warm and wondered if it would be improper if she suddenly took off for one of her walks.

As if reading her mind. "There's a bagel shop a few blocks away. Maybe we could grab something and take a walk around the lake that's nearby?" Matt asked.

"I'm not even hungry." Unfortunately, her stomach took this time to remind her that she'd only had coffee for breakfast this morning.

Matt cocked an eyebrow, looking at her smugly. "So, lunch?"

It was only lunch, and for the most part, Matt seemed harmless. If he had remained at Dalsin's and Son, the two of them might have shared a few lunches together. Trudy conceded and followed Matt out of the office. She checked around as she left to see if anyone was staring at the two of them, questioning why they would be together. But no one seemed to notice, and Mr. Dalsin was probably in his office eating his own lunch.

When they got outside, Matt produced a fob from his pocket, and pressed a button that emitted a beep, unlocking the doors of a very sleek sports car. Trudy knew the car had to be a rental, but just one day must have cost a fortune.

Matt walked to the passenger side of the car and opened the door for her. When he climbed into the driver's seat, he immediately stepped on the brake, cranked the car, and fled out of the parking lot.

Trudy was grateful there were no customers nearby. "Are we in a hurry?"

"Sorry," said Matt, sheepishly. "I forget how much horsepower this car has. Won't happen again."

They pulled into the parking lot where the bagel shop was located. Along with the bagel shop, there was one of those mass coffee chains, a deli, a mobile phone store, and a wine bar. They were lucky to have found a parking space at all; a short line had formed outside the coffee shop.

As they maneuvered around the people standing along the sidewalk, Matt hurried ahead to hold the door open for Trudy. She stepped inside and was immediately welcomed by the smell of the warm bagels baking in the back of the store.

Though it appeared that everyone in town was in need of caffeine this afternoon, there were only a few customers in line inside the shop. Trudy had already begun checking the time on her activity tracker, worried about what Mr. Dalsin would say when he didn't see her in her office. She should have let him know she was leaving.

"You can relax. I should have told you earlier, but I already spoke to Mr. Dalsin about taking you out to lunch."

"What," said Trudy, staring at him wide-eyed. "Why didn't you say something? I've been anxious this whole time."

"I can tell," Matt chuckled. "You looked like you were about to take off and walk back to the office any minute."

"And?" asked Trudy.

"And, what?" Matt responded.

Trudy, already agitated, was about to reach her breaking point. "The reason you didn't mention speaking with Mr. Dalsin."

"Oh, that. I thought it might add a little excitement to your day. You know, shake things up."

There was that phrase again.

"I would appreciate it if you wouldn't…." Trudy realized that her voice had started to rise, and they were getting looks from some of the people sitting at the tables nearby. She lowered her voice. "Put me in this situation again."

"Again?' Matt lifted one eyebrow. "Will there be *an* again?"

Had he not heard anything else she'd said? Evidently, his tendency for hearing what he wanted to, had helped him in business, but she was starting to see why there had not been any mention of a significant other, listed with his profile information on his website.

Never mind, it was just lunch. He would be gone soon enough, and her stomach was reminding her why they came here in the first place.

Trudy shook her head and got in line to order her bagel.

When it was her turn, she ordered her favorite, turkey and cheddar on a toasted sundried tomato bagel. Matt ordered an everything bagel with extra jalapeño cream cheese.

When it was time to pay for her order, Matt blocked her hand before she could give the cashier her bank card.

"I asked *you* out to lunch, remember?" Matt looked at the young man behind the counter. "Both orders are together."

Shrugging, she placed the card back in her wallet.

Matt grabbed the bags as they headed outside. "Ready for that walk?"

"Sure," Trudy squared her shoulders. "Since I see that my

day has already been planned for me."

Although it was the beginning of spring and Trudy's favorite time of year, this was the first day in a while that had been pleasant. The few trees planted along the lake were in full bloom, and a small breeze rustled the lime-colored leaves, playing them like piano keys. A small gust blew through the man-made fountain in the center of the lake, spraying droplets of water against their skin.

The day seemed too nice to spend indoors, making Trudy wish she were able to skip work and spend the day picnicking by the lake instead.

As they strolled along the lake, eating their bagels, Trudy noticed that Matt was several inches taller than she. The top of her head met the curve of his shoulders. Today, he had opted for a blue polo, khaki slacks, and loafers. With half of his arms exposed, she could see the corded muscles that the suit had hinted at yesterday. The hand holding his bagel was about twice the size of her own and held the appearance of someone who spent time with a manicurist. Even though Matt's legs were longer, he shortened his stride to match hers. He seemed to be enjoying the day as much as she was.

Because the shop had been extra generous with Matt's cream cheese, some of it lingered at the corners of his lips. Trudy watched as the tip of his tongue flickered out, licking the cheese away. The simple act, aroused feelings in her that had long remained dormant. She quickly looked away, feeling a sense of shame.

The lake was a lot more active than it used to be when she first started working at the hardware store. Back then, there had only been the bagel shop. And on the days she visited, she usually only had to share the lake with a few other people. Now, along with the extra shops, there was an additional section set aside for paddle boats.

A family was standing on the small pier near the boats.

The father was securing the life jackets of his two kids, a boy and a girl, while the mother stood back, filming them with her phone while shouting instructions.

The scene tugged at a sentimental chord within Trudy.

Paddle boarding was a fun activity her family often participated in when her kids were smaller.

"Something you'd like to try?" asked Matt, following her line of sight.

"Oh no," answered Trudy. "I was just thinking about how much things have changed."

"Me too," said Matt, staring at her intently.

Trudy was pretty sure they were not talking about the same thing. She quickly looked away from him and continued on their path.

"So, what have you been up to over the last few years?"

"Nothing much," answered Trudy. "Just life."

"Doesn't sound very exciting."

"Well, not all of us are meant to be the knight with hissteed, out here slaying dragons." Trudy waved her hands around dramatically.

"Does that make you the damsel in distress in need of saving?" Matt asked, a mischievous look in his eyes.

Why had he really come back?

That was an inappropriate question for a man to ask a married woman, but maybe he didn't know any better. Trudy halted in her steps. "Not saying you meant that comment in the way I took it. But just in case you did. You know I'm married. Right?"

Matt gazed off towards the lake for a second, then turned back to Trudy. "To answer your question, yes and yes. Yes,

I meant it in exactly the way you took it. And yes, I know you're married. I asked Mr. Dalsin."

"Well, if you knew that, why ask me to lunch? And why, you know…." Trudy wasn't sure of what she should call it. He hadn't exactly made a pass at her. His comments were more of…insinuations. "The rest of it."

"It *is* only lunch," Matt answered. "You could have said no. And as for the rest of it, as you put it. I find you attractive and wanted you to know."

"Okay," said Trudy hesitantly. "Thank you?"

"I think it's time I get you back to work."

"I think you're right," Trudy said, looking at the time.

Just remember to take things slow in that car of yours. Going too fast makes me nervous."

"Don't worry," said Matt, smiling down at her. "I'll take things slow."

Walking through her front door, Trudy was greeted with a sight that was so unfamiliar, she almost thought she was in the wrong house.

James and both her kids were sitting around the kitchen island eating pizza. The television in the living room was turned to one of those reality TV shows that Cori loved. The woman on the screen was yelling, pointing a dangerously sharp, bright yellow fingernail in the face of another woman.

Just days ago, she had wished for this exact same thing— well, not the reality show—but to sit down and share a meal with her kids. James was an added bonus. She rushed over to him, nearly pulling him out of his chair, and smushed a kiss against his cheek.

He braced himself in time, staring at Trudy, confused.

"It's nice to see you too."

"Hi, Mom, you're late," said Eric.

Cori looked up from the phone, eyeing her smartly. "Seems to be becoming a habit."

"Something came up. I had to stay later than usual." Trudy responded.

Coming home late was not customary for Trudy. Fortunately for her, her family thought her job was boring, so no one bothered to ask what that something was. She would have hated lying.

"Did anyone save me any?" Trudy lifted the lids of the takeout boxes and saw that they were empty.

"Dad bought a small barbecue chicken pizza just for you." Eric chimed in, pointing at a box on top of the stove.

"He did, did he?" Trudy looked at her husband, smiling, "Thanks, babe."

It was touching that James had thought enough to purchase her favorite pizza. Part of her wanted to ask where the money had come from, but she didn't want to ruin this rare occasion. It had become uncommon for James to be so considerate. She felt a pang of guilt as she remembered her lunch date.

"After getting my check this week and depositing it in the bank, I figured we deserved a little treat."

Thank God. One less thing to worry about. Maybe after the kids went off to their rooms, she and James could have some alone time.

Trudy settled down at the island with the rest of the family and placed a slice of pizza on a paper plate. "So, how was everyone's day?"

Mumbled *okays* came from her kids, who were too engrossed in their cell phones to bother looking up.

"My day was pretty much the same," answered James.

"Nothing much changes in the air-conditioning business. You mentioned something came up. How was your day?"

Suddenly, not as hungry as she had been seconds ago, Trudy placed the slice of pizza back on the plate. "Oh, that." She mulled over the best way to explain her day. "Well, an old coworker came into town and asked Mr. Dalsin and me to join him for lunch."

She knew it was only partially the truth, but what else could she say? *A handsome man asked her out to lunch?* It had been harmless, at least on her part. But spending time with a single man wasn't the same as hanging out with Shawna.

"Who was it?" James questioned casually.

"What?" asked Trudy.

"Who was the old coworker?"

Any other time, James seemed indifferent to her life outside the home. Why so curious now?

"It's not anyone you would know. He left not too long after I started working there."

"Then why would he ask you to lunch with Mr. Dalsin?"

Trudy was starting to feel like this was the point when she should ask for her lawyer.

"I think he was just trying to be nice. Mr. Dalsin was in my office when he suggested it."

James seemed satisfied with her answer and went back to eating his pizza.

"I think I'll go upstairs and get out of these clothes." Trudy tossed the unfinished pizza in the garbage.

"I'll be up soon," said James. "Maybe we can watch a movie or something."

"Sure, I'll take a quick shower, then meet you in bed."

Eric looked up from his phone, regarding them both unfavorably. "Yuck."

"Get your mind out of the gutter," Trudy yelled down the stairs, teasing.

As soon as she walked into the bedroom, she began stripping out of her clothes, tossing them in a nearby hamper. She switched on a light and began rummaging through her underwear drawer, looking for something suitable for a night in with her husband. After searching for what seemed like forever, Trudy began to think that she didn't own anything ideal until she found a black teddy tucked away in a back corner. The sheer, nylon teddy was etched in lace, with thin straps that crossed in the back. Perfect. It must have been years since she wore it.

Standing under the showerhead, Trudy let the warm water pour down over her. If not for the anticipation of spending some quality time with her husband, she would gladly stand there all day. She reached over and grabbed a scented body wash that James had once complimented her on, hoping it hadn't lost its essence since she last used it.

After stepping out of the shower, she wiped the condensation from the mirror and contemplated if she should do something with her hair. She piled it on top of her head, holding it in place with a clamp, and stood at the mirror, examining her features. In front of her stood a woman with what she would consider average looks. Average but not unappealing. She cupped her breast. They were a decent size and were *almost* where they should be. She smoothed her hand over her abdomen, testing the firmness. Not too bad for a mother of two.

Deciding that she would leave her hair in the clip, Trudy stepped inside the teddy, posed in front of the mirror, and decided she liked what she saw. Hopefully, James would as well.

She grabbed a robe, hanging from the back of the bathroom door, to cover up. It had been so long since they made love; she felt a little apprehensive walking out of the bathroom in just lingerie.

James was already in bed, scrolling through the shows saved on the DVR. It had been ages since they watched TV together. The saved list was at a hundred percent, and some of the episodes had been deleted for space.

She climbed into the bed and moved to the center to be close to James. "Have you settled on something we can watch?"

"You smell nice." James leaned over, sniffing close enough that his nose tickled the sensitive skin on her neck.

"Mm." Trudy moaned involuntarily.

"I forgot how crazy that makes you get." Reaching up, he released her hair from the clamp, lightly running his fingers up the back of her neck, pressing her head forward, bringing her closer to him. He began planting kisses up and down the back of her neck, sucking gently as he went.

Trudy felt her body jerk involuntarily. She instinctively placed her hand against his chest to push him away, not sure if she could handle all the sensations overwhelming her all at once.

James shook his head, grabbed her hand, and began moving it lower. He quickly pulled away to remove his shirt, eliciting a small whimper from Trudy. He tossed the shirt on the floor and quickly drew her back to him, this time, placing his lips on top of hers.

Ring. Ring.

Whose phone was that? Trudy felt James pulling away.

She placed her hand against his cheek to bring him back, back into this moment. "Let it ring," she whispered against his lips.

"I can't. It's the job."

He was right. No one else would be calling at this time of night. Both the kids were home.

"Please don't answer it. I miss you," Trudy pleaded.

"But you'd miss the money more," he snapped.

Trudy drew back as if she'd been slapped. Whatever she had been feeling was no longer there. She reached down, cinching her robe closed. James noticed the teddy underneath but said nothing. Instead, he answered the phone, taking it with him into the walk-in closet, where he kept his work clothes.

When he came out, Trudy was pretending to watch TV and refused to acknowledge him.

"Sorry for what I said. Maybe…we can take up where we left off…tomorrow?" James stood quietly waiting for an answer.

Trudy refused to respond, knowing she would begin sobbing if she tried to speak.

"Goodnight," he said before closing the bedroom door behind him.

When the door closed, the tears came. And they came in waves. All the frustration she'd been bottling up over the years, all the disappointment over feeling like she was doing it all alone, came flooding out of her. She muffled her cries in her pillow, afraid that her kids would hear her.

Why would he say something so hurtful after the moment they just shared? She had made it a point not to bring up money tonight, but he had still shoved it in her face.

Trudy reached over to her nightstand and grabbed her phone.

"Hello?"

"Shawna!" Trudy wailed.

"Girl, what's wrong? What happened?"

Suddenly, Trudy wasn't so sure if she wanted to confide in her friend. Even though she knew Shawna would take her side, she must be tired of hearing Trudy complain about her marriage. Trudy cleared her throat and tried for a cheerier tone. "I just called to say hey."

"You're not fooling anybody. Talk to me."

"Me… me… me, and James were finally connecting after all this time and, and…his phone rang."

"Okay…and then…What happened?" When Trudy didn't answer, Shawna put the pieces together. "Don't tell me he answered it?"

"Yesss…"

"I know that can't be everything. Something else must have happened to make you so upset."

"It was his job, but I asked him to stay, and he said…he said that I cared more about the money than being with him."

A gush of air vibrated against the phone's earpiece as Shawna exhaled. "If you weren't my friend, I would have some choice words to say about your husband, but I'm going to be nice. Do you need me to come by? I can help throw his stuff out."

Her friend's remarks suddenly made Trudy feel defensive. "No, Shawna, nobody's throwing anybody's stuff out. I just needed to call instead of lying here feeling sorry for myself."

"*Maybe* you should start to think about yourself for once.

Nobody else is." Shawna scoffed.

"I know. It's just that…I was so happy when I came in tonight and saw that the whole family was here, everybody together. I thought that it was a sign that—"

"A sign that what?" Shawna cut in. "That your kids were five again, and your husband finally noticed you were a human being with needs? When are you going to realize that your kids don't need you like they used to, and your husband is an idiot?"

Trudy sat silent. Even though she knew what Shawna said was true, part of her wanted to lash out and point out how imperfect Shawna's marriage was as well. To ask her; who was she, to ridicule *her,* to judge *her*, when she, herself, had no room to talk. But she knew she wouldn't. If she alienated Shawna, who would she have then?

"Trudy, are you still there?"

"Yes," Trudy said, sounding even more defeated than she had at the beginning of the call. I'm still here."

"I'm sorry if I sounded harsh. I know you called me for a shoulder to cry on, but your life isn't going to change until you work on the things that you have control over."

"You're right, Shawna. I'm going to go now and try and catch up on some missing sleep."

"You're not mad at me, are you?"

"No, and even if I was, it wouldn't be for long. Love ya, bye."

It was a beautiful day for yardsaling. Clear skies and a perfect 70°. Beads of dew were still clinging to the grass when Trudy headed out that morning. James was lying in bed beside her when she awoke. She wasn't sure when he had come in. It must have been sometime after she drifted off, because she had spent most of her night lying awake. Shawna's niggling words had taken precedence over sleep. She had finally given in and made up her mind to get out of the house to go and do something she loved.

Getting up early had allowed her the opportunity to be one of the first at many of the yard sales—some people were still setting up when she got there—allowing her the good fortune to unearth the better treasures. Sadly, she ended up giving away her discoveries to the people who could afford them. It was still nice to peruse the wares and imagine where she would have put everything once she took them home.

At one house, she'd found a beautiful bookcase that would have been a perfect match for her desk. She had nearly cried when she saw the couple who had purchased it loading it into their truck. She had been rummaging through a box at another home and found an oil painting much like Van Gogh's, A *Road at Saint-Remy with Female Figure*. It was almost an exact likeness, except the artist had included a small child walking alongside the female in the painting. It had only been priced at thirty-five dollars.

Trudy looked up to find another woman admiring it over her shoulder. She quickly asked if Trudy was going to buy it. She shook her head no and handed it over.

By the time Trudy made it home, everyone was up. She could hear music coming from Cori's bedroom, and Eric was sitting in front of the television, eating a bowl of cereal, watching an animated show.

"Hey, Mom, where have you been?"

"I went to a couple of yard sales."

Eric paused the show and turned to her. "You're doing that again? What'd you get?"

"Oh, nothing. It was more like window shopping. But I did see a lot of things I wanted."

"Why didn't you get them then?" Eric asked, confused.

Trudy had never let on to Eric and Cori about their finances. As far as they knew, they were doing fine financially. She didn't want to worry them about such things. She felt their jobs were to concentrate on schoolwork and being kids.

"Somebody else got to them first," Trudy responded.

"Better luck next time," he said, shrugging his shoulders and pushing play on the remote, returning to his show.

Trudy started the coffee in preparation for Cleaning Day. Most of her Saturdays were spent cleaning the house from top to bottom, and her insistently demanding for Eric to clean his room.

James came downstairs as she was finishing her cup of coffee. He walked over to her with his arms outstretched. Trudy turned around, facing the sink to avoid the embrace, and began washing out the coffee mug.

She felt James's arms as he wrapped them around her. She wanted to give in. More than anything, she needed the security that his embrace offered, but not from him. At least not today. She remained resistant until he gave up and moved away.

"Did you make *me* any coffee?" James asked.

"Nope."

"I see you're still mad at me."

Trudy spun around, leaned against the counter, and crossed her arms in front of her. "And you thought I wouldn't be?"

"It was work," James said as if that explained everything.

Trudy wanted to yell at him. Tell him how hurtful his

actions and words were to her last night, but she was tired of arguing. It seemed like all she did was talk about how everyone else's actions affected her, and it got her nowhere. What was the point?

"You know what, you're right. Your job is important, and I should understand that."

James regarded her for a second as if deciding if she was sincere or not. "Great, then everything is okay between us, and we can go back to normal?"

Sure, back to normal.

"Everything's okay." Trudy scrunched up the corners of her mouth.

"I thought I'd pick up some things for dinner tonight Anything you want in particular?"

Trudy shook her head. This was James's usual Saturday routine. If he wasn't working, he found a way to conveniently get missing, and didn't return until all the housework was completed.

James swept his keys from the kitchen counter and leaned forward, attempting to kiss Trudy on the lips. She turned her head, giving him her cheek. "Okay," he said, giving her a half-smile. "Be back soon."

Sure, you will.

Trudy collapsed onto her bed with a sigh of relief. She had just finished mopping, leaving the kitchen for last, and was done cleaning for the day. She had been tempted to lie down on the sofa but had pushed herself to come upstairs instead. Trudy didn't want to be downstairs when James came back with dinner. She didn't think she had it in her to cook anything tonight. The whole house, including her, smelled like bleach, and she just needed to take a little break. She would just close her eyes for a minute before changing out of her clothes.

Trudy was surprised to find yellow orchids sitting on her desk when she walked into her office Monday morning. At first, she thought they were from James. Yellow was her favorite color, and orchids were one of her favorite flowers. Although there had not been any more arguments over the weekend, there also had not been any effort from either of them to resume their activities from the previous night.

Unfortunately, any hope of the flowers being from James were immediately dispelled when she read the card.

I thought of you when I saw these. Thanks for lunch.— Matt.

Trudy sat down in her chair heavily, tapping the card against her desktop. She wondered what she should do about Matt and the flowers. She thought she had made it clear how she felt when they last spoke, that his intentions were unwelcome. He had simply driven her back to the hardware store, said goodbye as she got out of the car, and driven off. But then again, maybe he had listened, and the flowers were an apology, as she assumed they were when she thought they were from James.

And if the flowers were meant as an apology, there wouldn't be any harm in keeping them. Besides, regardless of Matt's intent, the orchids were innocent in all of this, and she couldn't see herself giving them away or tossing them in the trash.

Trudy was writing down a few notes of things to take care of after her lunch break, when she heard a tap on her door. She looked up to see Matt smiling at her.

"I see you got my flowers."

"Yes, I did, and thank you," she said, returning the smile. "I would have called, but I didn't have your number."

"I would have given it to you the other day, but I got the feeling you wouldn't have taken it."

Trudy got up from her desk and went to the door. "If that was everything," she said, ignoring his comment. "I was headed out to lunch. It was nice seeing you again." She held out her hand to shake his goodbye.

"No, it's actually not. I stopped by to take you out to lunch again."

Trudy dropped her hand. *Was he serious?* Guess she should have gotten rid of the orchids.

"I don't think that would be a good idea."

Matt reached out to grab the hand she'd offered earlier, pulling her towards him. "Why not? It is only lunch?" he whispered, looking down at her.

She knew she should pull away and yell at him for being so presumptuous, but her mind and body seemed frozen. She just stood there, staring up into his hazel eyes.

"I guess I'll take that as a…yes?" he asked, lifting one eyebrow. When Trudy didn't answer, he led her out of her office, still holding her hand. He did not let go until they were in the hardware store where others could see them.

Trudy didn't find her tongue until she was strapped in the passenger seat, and Matt was already pulling into traffic.

"You know you can't keep showing up like this, asking to take me out to lunch. People might start thinking something is going on between the two of us."

Matt shrugged his shoulders. "So what?"

"It doesn't look right for a married woman to be making lunch dates with a single man."

Matt took his eyes off the traffic for a second to study her face. "Are you worried about Mr. Dalsin firing you? I don't think going to lunch with me would be grounds for termination," he said, grinning. "Besides, if he did, you could come work for me."

"No, it's," Trudy stopped to search for the right word. "It's morally wrong. The people at the hardware store know me, and they know that I am married. It's just not right."

"What's wrong with two old friends catching up? It would only be wrong if your intentions towards me were less than honorable."

Matt snuck a look over at her. Trudy was sure the look he gave her meant he was hoping that they were. Trudy quickly looked away and noticed that they were not headed towards the bagel shop as she had assumed was their destination.

"Where are we going?" she asked.

"I thought we would go someplace where we could sit down this time."

Trudy leaned back into her seat. She supposed sitting down in a restaurant would look better than the two of them strolling around a lake together. It would be more like a business lunch between colleagues.

The restaurant was not very crowded for the afternoon rush, and they were given a table as soon as they walked in. The hostess seated them at a booth with high backs secluding them from the other patrons.

This would be the perfect setting for a couple at the beginning of their relationship, hidden away, sneaking in kisses.

Where had that thought come from, Trudy mused?

She had waited for Matt to sit down first, before sliding into the booth opposite of him, just in case he'd had been thinking something similar.

Trudy tried studying the menu but could feel Matt's eyes on her. She finally settled on a salad before setting the menu down and giving him her full attention.

"Why are you staring at me?"

"I'm sorry. Was I?" asked Matt, feigning confusion.

Trudy waited, refusing to play his game.

"I was just thinking… how little you've changed since I left. You're still as beautiful now as you were then."

Trudy could feel her cheeks burning and was thankful when the waitress showed up. She ordered a salad and a glass of water. Matt, a steak, baked potato, and a glass of red wine.

Gathering up the menus, Matt handed them to the waitress. "Would you like something to drink other than water? You know you don't have to worry about being a cheap date. I can afford it," he smiled at her teasingly.

She *had* decided that she *should* start thinking about herself, and a glass of wine would be nice. "You know what, I will take a glass of Sauvignon Blanc."

Matt watched as the waitress walked away. "Not used to hearing someone tell you that you're beautiful, are you?"

Trudy couldn't remember the last time the word beautiful had been directed towards her, but she didn't want to get into that conversation. She wasn't sure where it would lead.

"That was kind of you to say. Thank you." Trudy responded.

"You sound as if I told you I like your earrings. But I guess that answers my question. You *are* beautiful, you know? One might even say sexy."

The way he said the word sexy sent a shiver through her, almost as if he'd touched her. Trudy should have been shocked by his words, but she found that she liked hearing them. It must be the ambiance created by the booths. She needed to change the subject.

"I see leaving Dalsin's & Son worked out well for you?"

Matt seemed reluctant to change the subject but answered her question anyway. "Yes, it did. I hated the circumstances that led to me receiving the money...." He trailed off as if recalling a painful memory but seemed to shake it off. "But it allowed me the opportunity to start the business I'd always wanted. My parents would have wanted it that way."

Trudy seemed to remember some talk, right before Matt left, about an inheritance or life insurance surrounding his parents' deaths. She had chalked it up to office gossip. But evidently, some of it must have been true.

"I'm sure they would have been proud of you. I saw the numbers from your last quarterly report."

"You've been checking up on me?" Matt asked, cocking his head to the side.

Trudy suddenly felt cornered. "I was just curious. I wasn't trying to snoop or anything."

"It's okay," said Matt, smiling at her. "I like knowing you are thinking about me when I'm not around."

Again, she was saved from having to respond, by the waitress who was returning with their drinks.

Trudy sipped her wine, wishing she had ordered something stronger. Wishing she had been able to talk her way out of having lunch with Matt.

"I can get the whole bottle if you like," Matt suggested.

"It's already bad enough that I left with you. I don't need to return to work drunk as well. You seem to be a bad influence on me."

"You say that like it's a bad thing."

The way he spoke and looked at her, made her feel as if she were naked. Trudy fought the urge to take her napkin and cover herself. She had purposely sat across from him, allowing distance, but it didn't seem to matter. If his words could make her feel this way, she wondered how it would feel if he made good on them.

"So, how long have you been married?"

Trudy was caught off-guard by the change in subject. "Um…almost twenty years."

"You have two kids, right?"

Trudy furrowed her brow, wondering about his line of questioning. "Yes, Cori, who is eighteen, and Eric, is fifteen."

"And your husband?"

"James."

"And how is married life?"

Trudy felt strange answering questions about her marriage. Before, she had used it as a shield to ward off Matt's advances. Now it felt wrong to talk about it with him.

"Well, as with anything in life, it takes work."

Trudy leaned back to allow the waitress to place their food in front of them. The waitress waited for Matt to cut into his steak to ensure it was the correct temperature before walking away.

Placing a portion of the meat into his mouth, he began to chew, and for a long moment, Matt seemed to be lost in thought. "Maybe that's the reason my past relationships didn't work out. Life is so hard. Who wants to work at something that should be so easy?"

"What makes you think relationships should be easy?"

asked Trudy.

"I don't know. I just figured that if you decide to marry someone, it would be a person who shares your same interests and desires. And if you are trying to accomplish the same goals, what is there to work on?"

Trudy didn't have an answer for him. Over the last few years, she had often asked herself the same question.

Instead of replying, she ate her salad in silence.

When Trudy returned to the hardware store, Mr. Dalsin was waiting for her at the entrance and walked with her to her office.

"How was lunch?" he asked.

Trudy scrunched her forehead. "Um…It was good. How was yours?"

"I see you spent it with Matt," Mr. Dalsin responded, ignoring her question.

"Yes. We were catching up while he's in town."

Mr. Dalsin stopped and turned towards her. "Was that all it was?"

Trudy knew people would begin to talk, but she didn't think anyone would be so bold as to come out and ask, especially Mr. Dalsin.

"What do you mean?"

Mr. Dalsin glanced around to see if anyone was nearby. "You know he came here to try to buy my company?"

Trudy was taken aback by his question. She knew that this could not have been a simple trip to reminisce with old coworkers, but she had no idea that Matt wanted to buy the hardware store. His business was doing well. Why would he want to buy a small Mom & Pop store?

"No, Mr. Dalsin. It never came up."

"I told him no. I thought maybe," he said, lowering his gaze. "His interest in you may have something to do with our finances."

Trudy placed her hand on his shoulder, hoping to offer some reassurance. "I would never do that. I am loyal to you and this company."

He returned her gaze and appeared to be convinced. "I should have known better. I'm sorry."

"You don't need to apologize. I would have thought the same if I were in your shoes."

Mr. Dalsin nodded and walked away, down the hall to his office, muttering to himself.

CHAPTER 3

TRUDY HAD SPENT the better part of the day thinking about Mr.Dalsin's confrontation. She had woken up this morning before the alarm clock, and walked Blue before making sure the kids got off to school. She hadn't been prepared for the reprimand she had already assumed was coming to her. She was even less prepared to learn about Matt's new business venture.

She wondered why he had never mentioned it to her, not that it was any of her business after hearing Mr. Dalsin had turned him down. But what was even more curious, if Mr. Dalsin had refused his offer and he wasn't after her for information, why was he still in town?

Now would be a good time to call Shawna and talk it over with her; as she did, any time she was faced with a puzzle she was at a loss to solve. But she wasn't in the mood for her friend's intrusive personality today.

She had picked up the phone a few times but quickly laid it back down. In order for her to tell Shawna about her conversation with Mr. Dalsin, she would have to confess the reasons behind Mr. Dalsin's suspicions. Her lunch dates with Matt. And she could only imagine what Shawna would have to say about that.

Worrying about all of this was going to give her a headache. She was looking through the kitchen cabinet for aspirin, when James came home.

He seemed perplexed to see her standing there. "Hey, thought you slept in or something. I was surprised when I didn't see you and Blue in the driveway."

As if on cue, Blue ran over to James and began rubbing against his leg. James quickly shooed the dog away. Instead of leaving, Blue sat down, staring up at him, but quickly ran off when James ordered him to his cage.

"Come here, Blue," Trudy called the dog over to her, petting him. Why had James even wanted a dog in the first place? He clearly only saw him as a nuisance. "I woke up a little earlier than usual and took him out."

"Something on your mind?"

She had not considered talking it over with James, but he was her husband, her helpmate. She could try discussing Matt's business plans without bringing up the rest of it.

"Remember when I told you about the coworker who came into town?"

"Yeah, the one who took you out to lunch." James crossed his arms in front of him.

"Took both me *and Mr. Dalsin* out to lunch," Trudy corrected, remembering the fib she had told. "Well, it seems that his visit wasn't for leisure, he was interested in buying the hardware store."

James shrugged. "What's wrong with that? You are always saying the store is doing well."

"I don't know. It's just that Mr. Dalsin thought I was in on it."

James eyed her suspiciously. "Why would he think

something like that?”

Trudy hadn't thought this through. No matter how she spun it, she would have to enlighten James about Matt's interest in her. “Well… it's just that Matt asked about me before he came back, and he has come by the office a few times to see me.”

“To see *you*,” asked James pointedly.

“He kind of let me know that he was interested in me….” Seeing that James was about to respond, Trudy hurried and added. “But I let him know I was married.”

“So, Mr. Dalsin thought he was coming to get information from you because you handle the books. Right?

“Right,” answered Trudy.

“And it bothers you that Mr. Dalsin would think that way about you?”

“Yes, I consider myself to be trustworthy, and I would hope that anyone who knew me, would think the same way.”

At least where my job is concerned.

With the emotions Matt had begun to stir in her, she was starting to feel that her marriage may be a different story.

“I wouldn't worry about it. If Mr. Dalsin told him no, and he's not trying to fish any information out of you, he should be leaving town soon. Unless there is something else keeping him here?” James raised an eyebrow questioningly.

“No, no. He should be leaving soon. There shouldn't be anything else keeping him here. I mean, how would I know?”

“If there's not anything else you want to run by me, I'm going to go lie down. Hope things get better at work. I'm sure things will be back to normal in no time.”

James walked away, leaving Trudy even more confused than she was before their conversation. Should she be worrying about what James was thinking? If he was worried about Matt being a threat, he didn't show it.

What would he think if he knew Matt had called her sexy? Would he still have gone upstairs to lie down or asked to meet the man who had dared to speak to his wife that way?

Still unable to come to terms with everything that was going on and working off little sleep, Trudy decided she would stay and work from home today. Most of the work she had to do could be done from home anyway. She could access her work computer from her laptop.

She picked up her phone and dialed Mr. Dalsin's assistant's direct line.

"Hello, Dalsin's & Son, how may I direct your call?"

"Hi, Peggy, it's Trudy."

"Hi, Trudy, how are you?" Peggy replied cheerfully.

Although there was nothing physically wrong with her, Trudy didn't want to seem too chipper on the phone; she slowed her words, hoping to sound unwell. "Okay, but I was calling to let Mr. Dalsin know I wouldn't be in the office today and would be working from home."

"Is everything okay?" Peggy asked, seemingly concerned. "Mr. Dalsin told me about your talk yesterday. He was really upset about accusing you. I hope it hasn't caused you to feel unwelcome here."

"Oh, no, and it's nothing like that. I told him I understood why he was asking."

"Just to let you know, I would have never thought anything like that about you," added Peggy conspiratorially.

Trudy knew that Peggy would keep her on the phone all day if she could. "Thank you, Peggy. I really appreciate that. You have my home number if anyone needs me." She hung up.

As if sensing the time, Blue walked into his cage, turned

around, and waited for Trudy to engage the latch to close him in before heading to work.

"Not today, Buddy. You get to hang out as much as you want."

He sat for a moment. After seeing that she made no movement toward him, he walked out of the cage and into the mudroom.

Smart dog, she thought, as she followed behind him.

It had been easy to log into the hardware store's computer, allowing Trudy to complete most of her work. Unfortunately, a few times, she found her mind wandering back to the whole hardware dilemma. During those occasions, she got up, stretched, and walked outside, hoping the sunlight would help her to refocus.

It was starting to appear that staying home had not helped. The more she tried to ignore the things happening in her life, the more they kept needling their way back in.

Just as she was getting up for another one of her breaks, she heard her phone ring. The number on the screen was unfamiliar; maybe one of the kids was calling from a friend's phone.

"Hello?"

"Hi. How are you today?"

So much for trying to clear her head. "Matt?"

"Yes."

"How'd you get this number?"

"You don't sound too happy to hear from me," he said, sounding bemused.

"Well, just wondering how you got my number, since I'm pretty sure I don't remember giving it to you."

"Oh, well, about that. I went by the store, and you weren't there, so, I talked to Peggy, and she said you were working from home today."

"And…I'm guessing she's the one that gave you my number?" Trudy shook her head. "So, what is it I can do to help you?"

"Is everything okay? You seem to be upset with me. And it seems like it's more than just about me having your number."

"Oh, nothing…*besides causing friction in my workplace.*" Trudy snapped.

"I don't understand. How could *I* have done that? Was it our lunch dates?"

"Yes, but not in the way you think. Mr. Dalsin thought you were pressing me for information about the company. Seeing that you were just trying to buy it a few days ago."

"Oh."

"Seems like you might have let me in on this, so I didn't get blindsided."

"I would have assumed Mr. Dalsin would have already discussed that with you."

"Well, he didn't," said Trudy, feeling defensive.

"I'm sorry if my spending time with you has caused problems with you and Mr. Dalsin, but I would hope that you know our lunches had nothing to do with the company. It's not the way I do business."

It was true that the hardware store had never come up during their time together, but she just wished someone

would have told her what was going on. Maybe then, she would have gone out of her way to avoid Matt.

"I don't know what *I* know right now."

"Normally, I would be offended, but you are right. We don't know each other, which is why I called. Are you free for lunch?"

"What?"

"How else can we get to know each other?"

One thing about Matt, he was persistent. She knew she should say no, but this could be the opportunity to find out a little more about why Matt wanted to buy the hardware store, and why he was still in town after Mr. Dalsin had turned him down.

"Sure, where do you want to meet?"

Matt was silent on his end. Probably shocked that she had given in so quickly.

"Why don't I come by and pick you up?"

"You don't understand discretion, do you? No. My husband is home."

"Really?" Matt asked. "I'd love to meet him."

"No. You wouldn't." Trudy was starting to get frustrated. "Where do you want to meet?" she asked, slowly emphasizing each word.

Evidently realizing he had gone too far, Matt relayed the address, telling her he would see her in a few before hanging up the phone.

Trudy hoped she was dressed appropriately for the restaurant they were meeting at. She could not risk going upstairs to change. James didn't even know she had stayed home, and she wasn't in the mood to be interrogated again.

She typed the address into her phone and took Blue out to relieve himself before putting him in his cage. "Sorry," she said, giving him a soulful look. She grabbed her keys and headed out.

Trudy spotted Matt's car as soon as she pulled into the restaurant's parking lot. He got out of his car and started walking over as she backed into a parking space.

As soon as Trudy got out of the car, Matt caught her

around her waist. "This is something I have been wanting to do for a long time." He pulled her to him, crushing his lips to hers.

She knew she should put a stop to this. What if someone saw them? She tried to resist—at least she thought she did—but her body seemed to have a mind of its own, and it melted into him as she gave in.

His tongue flitted across her lips, demanding its way in, and she opened her mouth, allowing him entry. Her hand reached up, pulling his head closer as she kissed him back.

Suddenly, he pulled away, looking down at her, grinning. "That was better than anything I could have imagined."

Trudy wasn't sure if it was the abrupt end to the kiss or the fact that he had dared to kiss her in the first place, but she was unsettled and a bit mortified. "How. How dare you? Have you lost your mind!?"

Matt regarded her curiously. "Correct me if I'm wrong, but you seemed to have enjoyed it. Did you not?"

"No, I didn't." Trudy raged.

"And…you're sure about that?" he asked, lifting one eyebrow.

"No, I mean yes. Yes, I'm sure." She turned around and opened her car door. "I should have never come."

Matt placed his hand against the door, stilling her movements. "Come on, this is unnecessary. It was just a kiss."

"A kiss I didn't agree to. A kiss with me, a married woman." Trudy looked around. "Someone could have seen."

"That's why I picked this restaurant—someplace out of the way," Matt said as if he was congratulating himself.

"So, you planned this little seduction?"

He looked at her as if he were observing a small child.

"Really, Trudy? What did you think all these lunch dates were really about?"

Now, she felt even more ashamed. "I don't know about those other times, but *today, I thought* we could talk about why you were trying to buy the hardware store and why you never told me about it."

"That had nothing to do with you." Matt retorted.

"No?" she asked, staring up at him. "What about my job?"

He shook his head. "Nothing would have changed. I just felt Mr. Dalsin would be happy to have a reason to retire, and I am in a position to make that happen. And as far as your job is concerned, it would have been safe."

She felt even more foolish. "Thanks. I appreciate you alleviating my concerns, but I have to go now. Please let go." Trudy tugged on the door handle.

Although it appeared he was reluctant to do so, Matt released the door. He stepped back and watched her drive away.

It was about a mile down the street when Trudy pulled over to the side of the road. She smacked her hands against the steering wheel repeatedly. "You idiot."

How could she be so stupid? She knew Matt was interested in her. Why had she allowed herself to be placed in this position in the first place? Why did she believe she could keep meeting him, without him eventually assuming, she had felt the same way? Or had she been kidding herself?

She could not lie. She found Matt attractive, which was even more reason to avoid him. But she had to admit, it was hard not to seek out the attention that she craved. Even harder when she wasn't getting it at home.

After that kiss—Trudy's fingers unconsciously went to her lips—she could no longer pretend it was a simple attraction. Even now, she longed to know him more. The way he tasted was intoxicating.

All these years, she had remained faithful to her marriage. What was it about Matt that she had allowed him to get this close? And this fast? It could not just be the problems in her marriage. Other men had shown interest in her in the past, and nothing had ever come of it.

She even found him to be infuriating at times, but each time he called, she came. As much as she had tried to avoid it, there was only one person she knew she could turn to.

Trudy knew she was taking a chance showing up unannounced. Although she had been to Shawna's house many times over the years, her visits had started to become less frequent. And even though Greg should still be away, she wasn't sure how Shawna would react to her showing up out of the blue.

The doorbell played a little melody as she held down the button. When no one answered after a few seconds, Trudy placed her ear against the door, listening. There were faint sounds of the television coming from inside the house. Shawna's car was still in the driveway, but that did not necessarily mean she was home.

Trudy raised her fist to knock at the door when it opened. Her friend stood in front of her wearing a terry cloth robe, blinking and shielding her eyes against the sunlight.

"Trudy?"

"Sorry. Did I wake you?" asked Trudy apologetically.

"Just taking an afternoon nap." Shawna opened the door

to let Trudy in. "Why didn't you call first?"

"I know I should have, but I needed to talk, and I wasn't sure if I could drive at the same time."

"Well, have a seat. You want something to drink?"

By the way Shawna asked the question, Trudy knew she meant something stronger than water. "Tea if you got it—"

Just then, her stomach grumbled. Lunch *had* been postponed, "And maybe something to snack on."

Shawna gave her a look before heading off to the kitchen.

Although Shawna did not work, she and Greg did well for themselves. Ebony hardwood floors ran throughout the entirety of the house. All the appliances had been recently updated. The soft plush sofa that Trudy was currently sitting on, held giant sumptuous pillows that attempted to suck you in if you leaned back too far. A massive coffee table sat in the middle of the living room. Underneath the glass that lay on top of it, was an intricate etching of what appeared to be a rainforest. Shawna had once mentioned, that the table had been purchased when Greg was stationed overseas.

Trudy leaned back into the sofa and reflected over how different their lives had changed since middle school. They had become fast friends back then, bonding over their shared dysfunctional childhoods. Both grew up in households where they had been left to raise themselves, by parents who were more concerned with working and partying than paying attention to their teenage daughters.

After high school, Trudy went to Business school, and Shawna married Greg, who joined the military not too soon after. They stayed in touch by writing to each other over the years, before Shawna and Greg eventually returned to the States after his tours were over.

Shawna reappeared with a coffee mug filled with warm

tea and some shortbread cookies. "So, what's got you so crazy, you'd show up without calling first?"

After a moment of trying to decide where to start, Trudy gave up and allowed the whole story to spill from her. Beginning with the lunch dates, then on to Mr. Dalsin's accusations, and ending with the kiss today. Once she had said everything aloud, she felt somewhat lighter. She wished she had talked to Shawna sooner. As she waited for her friend to reply, Trudy took a sip of tea and began choking on the liquid. "What's in this?"

Shawna pounded on her back. "Just a little rum. I figured you could use it. Guess I should have warned you first."

Trudy placed the cup down. "Yeah, I think so."

Shawna eyed her curiously. "So, what are you going to do about it?"

"Do about what?"

"The kiss. Are you going to finish what was started?"

Trudy regarded her friend skeptically. "You mean, am I going to take things further with Matt?"

Shawna nodded her head.

"Aren't you supposed to be telling me how stupid I've been, and ask me how I could do something like this to my husband and kids?"

"I'm sure those are all the things you have already been telling yourself. You don't need me for that. I'm just saying. What would be the harm if something more were to happen? You deserve to have a little fun in your life."

Trudy gawked at her friend with her mouth open so long, that Shawna reached over and closed it for her. She had gone crazy. That was the only thing that made sense. People like Trudy didn't go around having one-night stands.

"Listen. What do you think I do when Greg is gone?"

Shawna asked nonchalantly.

"From the looks of you, I would think you sleep all day."

"Oh, this," said Shawna, looking down at her robe. "I went out last night, didn't get in until early this morning."

"And what *do* you *do* when you go out at night?" Trudy asked hesitantly.

"Sometimes, I meet men. Sometimes they buy me drinks. Sometimes, a little more happens. It's harmless."

Trudy tugged on her hair, trying to make sense of this. Her friend went out and slept with strangers. "And why is this the first time I'm hearing about this?"

"I'd thought about inviting you out with me a few times, but like you said, you have your husband and your kids."

"Does Greg know about this?" Trudy whispered.

Shawna looked at her and laughed. "Yeah, right. Girl, he would kill me."

"Then why do you do it?" Trudy questioned, unsure if she wanted to know the answer. It was one thing for Trudy to have feelings for a man she barely knew, but for her friend to sleep with random strangers, was another. The thought scared her.

Shawna took her time before answering, as if this was the first time she had ever thought about it. "He's just so controlling. I guess this is a way to get back at him, to have some control of my own, and it's kind of fun."

Evidently, there had been a lot going on in her friend's life that Trudy did not know about. The years they had spent apart had changed the girl she used to know. Who was this woman sitting in front of her, leading such a reckless life? The woman who was encouraging her to do the same. But, regardless of how Trudy felt about Shawna's current life decisions, it wasn't her right to judge. It was Shawna's life to lead, and she still needed Shawna in hers. Trudy would be there whether she supported her friend's decisions or not.

"This is a lot, Shawna."

"What, you gonna stop talking to me now?" she asked, sounding hurt and angry.

"No. Never. It's not for me to judge. Besides, who else do I have but you?" Trudy reached out to grab Shawna's hand. "I'm just worried. Isn't it kind of dangerous?"

Shawna softened a bit and smiled. "Maybe in the beginning, but now it's the same guy every time."

That made Trudy feel a little better. Just a little.

"I'm not saying you should go out here and start meeting random men like I did, but you've got this man who's interested. And clearly, you feel the same, or you wouldn't be over here crying on my shoulder. James doesn't have to find out, and if he did, you know, he would never leave you."

As she said, Trudy would never judge her friend, but she was not ready to put her marriage in jeopardy the way Shawna had, strangers or not.

She gave her friend a hug before grabbing up a handful of shortbread cookies on her way out of the house. Although it had taken a weight off of her to talk things over with Shawna, this was a conversation she needed to have with James.

All the things that were attracting her to Matt, the attention and the compliments, were the same things she could get at home. She would just have to let James know that he needed to step up and do a better job. Because if he didn't, then…Then what? There was no what. James would just have to listen this time so things could go back to the way they were supposed to be.

James was sound asleep in the center of the bed when Trudy walked into their bedroom. She did not want to wake him, but if she didn't have this conversation now, she knew she would never have the courage to bring it up again.

She contemplated leaving the room immersed in darkness while they spoke, but decided that would be the cowardly thing to do and turned on her bedside lamp.

"James."

Nothing.

She reached over, nudging his leg. "James?"

"What… what? What is it?"

"We need to talk."

He rubbed his eyes, staring at her, confused. "Now?"

"Yes. Now."

James sat up, propping the pillows behind him, and spread his hands in front of him as if to say, 'Go ahead.'

"I love you. You know that, right?"

James shrugged his shoulders. "Of course."

"The thing is, I have always been faithful to you and this marriage. But… recently, I've been getting attention from other men."

Trudy waited to see if James would respond. When he didn't, she continued, wringing her hands together. "I'm worried that this *attention* might eventually cause me to stray. Basically, what I am saying or asking, is that, if you could start to show me the same attention. You know, like how things used to be between us? So, I'm not…not tempted to cheat."

"So, what you're saying is, you need me to start giving you more attention?" James asked, appearing to be very annoyed.

Trudy nodded.

"Okay. Got it. So, is it okay if I go back to sleep now?"

Trudy's brow creased. "I guess?"

"Good, can you get that light?" James slid back down in the bed, throwing the cover back over him.

What the hell was that? Trudy thought as she closed the bedroom door behind her. She hadn't been sure how that conversation was going to go, but she definitely hadn't pictured it going like that.

Well, at least no one can say I didn't try.

CHAPTER 4

IT HAD BEEN FOUR days since her talk with James, and nothing much had changed. Later that night, he roused her from her sleep to tell her he loved her and kissed her on the forehead before leaving for work. But after that, things had gone back to how they always were. The distance between them was still there days later.

Trudy had considered making the first move, but that would have defeated the purpose. Wasn't the whole objective of their talk to get him to come to her, to make her feel wanted?

Sitting in front of her computer, working on the hardware store's tax documents, was not giving her the same comfort as it had in the past. Things with Mr. Dalsin had pretty much gone back to normal as well, but there was still the insinuation hanging over her head. She hoped that all this would soon blow over. The hardware store had always been her place of refuge, and she couldn't imagine if that was taken from her as well.

Matt had stopped showing up at her office. Her only contact from him had been a text message telling her if she ever needed to talk, she could call or come by his hotel fordrinks, along with an address for the hotel.

Trudy knew she should delete the text, but she didn't. Leaving it was dangerous, especially with James refusing to respond to her request, but she could not bring herself to get rid of it.

While she sat staring at the spreadsheet on her computer, her office phone rang.

"Hello, Trudy Allen."

"Hi, Mrs. Allen, this is the school nurse."

"Yes?" Trudy responded apprehensively.

"Your daughter Cori is in my office complaining of stomach pains. I think it might be that time of the month, but we are not allowed to give her anything."

"I'm on my way." Trudy hung up the phone.

She ran by Peggy's office to let her know she would be gone for the day, explaining she needed to pick Cori up from school. The older woman waved her away, telling her she understood and would let Mr. Dalsin know.

Hurrying to the car, Trudy realized she was probably being a bit excessive, especially if it was just cramps, but how often did her daughter need her? She had made sure to grab some pain medicine from her desk drawer and a bottle of water, to have on hand once she got to the school.

After signing in at the front desk and letting the receptionist know why she was there, Trudy was directed to the nurse's office.

The nurse's office was in stark contrast to the rest of the school. On her way to the office, the walls were covered in colorful decorative signs and posters announcing school events and important dates. Everything here was sterile and white, with the exception of the blacked-out computer screen, the nurse who greeted her, wearing green scrubs under a white lab coat, and her daughter Cori lying in the fetal position on an exam table in the corner.

Trudy thanked the nurse for calling her, then went over to Cori, placing her hand on her forehead. "How ya doing?"

"What, did you stop and get lunch or something?" Cori bit out.

"No. I got here when I could. There was a lot of traffic because it's lunchtime."

The nurse looked at her apologetically. "Cori is free to go."

"Thank you," said Trudy. "Cori, you ready to go? I brought some pain pills."

Cori turned to her, whispering, "I had an accident."

Trudy whispered back. "Well, let's get you home so you can get a bath and feel better. Okay?"

Cori looked at her reluctantly but swung her legs over the side of the table and stood up. "Can I get your jacket, please?"

Removing the jacket she was wearing, Trudy handed it to her daughter and watched as she tied it around her waist.

When they got to the car, she offered Cori some pain pills and water. After downing the pills, Cori leaned the car seat back and turned to face the window.

Trudy took her response to mean she didn't want to be bothered. She left Cori to her thoughts and drove home, listening to the radio.

When they got to the house, Cori was nearly up the stairs before Trudy could pull her key out of the lock. It wasn't long before the sounds of running water could be heard coming from the tub in the kids' bathroom. With Cori coming home early, Trudy needed to let Eric know his sister would not be riding the bus with him this afternoon.

While texting Eric, she was hit with the strong scent of urine and instantly knew what it was. Following the smell to Blue's cage, she saw that he had soiled the replacement pan and his bedding. He was crammed over in one of the corners, trying to avoid it.

"Great, this day just keeps getting better," muttered Trudy to herself as she cursed James for forgetting to take Blue out.

After tossing Blue's bedding in the wash, she spent the next thirty minutes cleaning his cage and washing him outside under the hose. Trudy went to throw the soiled paper towels she used into the trash can outside. As she opened the lid, she heard a chirping sound coming from inside. She paused for a second before tossing in the towels. Just as the lid was about to close, a tiny green frog jumped out, brushing past the side of her face. Yelling, she leapt back and started swatting frantically at her ear.

Once the creepy chills subsided and she determined the frog was no longer a threat, she sat down on the back stairs to calm herself.

Why was she doing this? Why was she acting as if this was what life was supposed to be like? Trudy felt as if she were an actor on stage, playing the part of a happy housewife. She was tired of playing the role. This couldn't *possibly* be what life was all about—everyone constantly taking and never giving back. Even after rushing to school today to be there for Cori, it had ended up backfiring. Instead of thanking her, her daughter had complained about how much time it took her to get there.

No good deed goes unpunished.

Walking back into the house, Trudy washed her hands, picked up her phone, and texted Matt to see if he wanted to meet for drinks. He instantly replied, 'Yes.'

Now, to get ready.

On her way upstairs, she tapped on the kids' bathroom door to check on Cori. Through the door. she could hear music coming from the Bluetooth speaker Cori kept in there.

"Everything okay in there?"

"Yes, Mom," said Cori, sounding annoyed and like her father. "Just soaking in the tub."

"Okay. Just letting you know I'm going out. Do you need anything before I go?"

"Just to be left alone," Cori said, drawing the words out.

Was it okay to sometimes not like your kids?

On any other day, Trudy tried to be considerate of James's sleeping, but today, she could care less. He couldn't be bothered enough to take Blue out, leaving her to clean up after him. So, she couldn't be bothered to make sure his sleep went uninterrupted. Besides, he had already told her he wouldn't be receiving a paycheck this week. Who cared if he was too tired to work for free?

She went into her closet to search for something to wear and quickly chose a yellow dress with a floral pattern she had not worn in years. It was most likely out of fashion, but she had always liked the way it suited her, accentuating all the right areas. She grabbed a pair of tan wedges that complemented the dress.

James did not stir when she walked past the bed on her way into the bathroom to take her shower. Trudy was sure he must have heard her come in, but if he wanted to pretend, so could she.

While she bathed, she would pretend that she wasn't going to meet Matt for drinks at his hotel. She could pretend that drinks *might* not lead to something else—to a decision that she may end up regretting later.

Had Shawna felt this same way her first time?

Trudy laid the dress on the countertop and stared in the mirror, remembering the last time she had readied herself to be with a man. On that occasion, she had been rejected. She wondered if she were to be refused this time, would she embrace it and be grateful to Matt for pushing her away?

In the shower, she groomed every area that had been neglected over the winter months. It had not seemed necessary to take such care, given the lack of intimacy between her and James, and having spent most of the season covered up.

Out of the shower, she dried off and wrapped the towel around her. Reaching out, she wiped the mist from the mirror.

"Maybe a little makeup."

Her makeup was in a see-through bag that was tossed in the back of a drawer. Most of it was dried and caked and no longer viable. Thankfully, she was able to find some lip gloss and eyeliner that had survived.

Pulling the dress over her head, she took care not to muss the lip gloss. She tied the sash loosely around her waist, then sprayed on a few drops of her favorite perfume behind her ears. After running a brush through her hair, Trudy stepped back to view herself.

"Not bad," she said aloud to herself.

The bartender was wiping down the counter as Trudy selected a stool at the bar.

"What can I get you to drink?"

Trudy wasn't sure how long she would be staying and didn't want to be intoxicated on her ride home, but she opted for a margarita with a top-shelf tequila. She would need the liquid courage if things progressed further than the bar.

She had sat in the car outside the hotel for about fifteen minutes before texting Matt to let him know she was here. His response had been for her to wait for him in the bar. He'd been on a business call.

While waiting for her drink, she looked around. Her eyes landed on the grand piano in the center of the room. A man wearing a tuxedo jacket sat on a bench, playing a slow medley with a snifter in front of him for tips. The majority of the bar's patrons appeared to be businessmen. Most of them were on their laptops or phones. Others were in groups of three or four, laughing and enjoying a few drinks together.

The bartender placed her drink down in front of her. She was just about to thank him as she reached into her purse to pay, when a man sat down beside her.

"Put it on my tab, Ron," he said as he handed the bartender his credit card.

Trudy opened her mouth to protest, but the bartender had already swiped the card before she could say anything.

The first thing she noticed about her companion was his expansive forehead. His combover was doing a pitiable job of covering what was left of his receding hairline.

"Thank you, but you didn't have to," said Trudy.

"You're more than welcome, young lady." The man smiled, extending his hand. "Hi, I'm Paul."

Trudy returned his handshake. "Hi, Paul. Trudy."

Paul engulfed her hand with his, latching on. "This is my first time seeing you here."

Trudy pulled away, wiping the sweat from Paul's hand on a cocktail napkin. "It's my first time coming here." She laughed nervously, confused by his comment.

"Well, that would explain it then."

She cocked her head, staring at him. Her conversation with Shawna suddenly resurfaced, and then understanding set in. Did he think—

"Hey buddy, I think you're sitting in my spot."

Both Trudy and Paul turned to find a very perturbed Matt standing behind them.

"I was here first. Maybe you can wait for the group that comes in a little later. Or?" Paul looked back at Trudy, a sly grin forming on his face. "You can have her when I'm –"

Before Paul could finish, he was aggressively yanked from his seat. About a foot shorter than Matt, Paul stood gaping up at him, mad-eyed.

"You can have her," Paul said, waving his hands in front of him. "It's not a big deal."

"This woman, who you have wrongfully mistaken for someone else, is a friend of mine, and I believe you owe her an apology." Matt spat out.

Paul looked at Trudy and then back at Matt. "I'm sorry, I didn't know. She should have said something."

Matt looked further annoyed and began squeezing and pressing down as he applied pressure to Paul's shoulder. "Now, let's try this again. Apologize to the lady and this time without blaming her in the process."

Trudy knew she must appear a fool sitting there with her mouth open, but she was confused as to what was going on. One minute, she was being propositioned, and the next, Matt was throttling the man.

"I said I'm sorry. Okay?" Paul looked at Trudy, pleading.

"Matt," she said, placing her hand on his back. "He's sorry. Let him go. Please."

Matt turned and looked at Trudy as if he'd forgotten she

was there. He released Paul, who ran off and sat down with a group of men at one of the tables, who had watched the whole incident unfold without intervening.

"Forgive me," said Matt, taking the seat beside her. "Are you okay?"

"Physically? Yes. But a little embarrassed. You didn't have to come to my rescue like that."

"Why not? Someone had to." Matt peered around the bar. Anyone catching his eyes quickly looked away.

Matt's comment touched her. As shocked and mortified as she'd been by the incident, it had been nice to have someone defend her honor for once. It reminded her of her remark about him being the knight on his steed slaying dragons, and his response that she was the damsel in distress in need of saving. Back then, she had been quick to reprimand him for being inappropriate, but now, that conversation was like a distant memory of an imaginary moment in time.

"You know what? I should be thanking you instead of worrying about what these people think." Trudy met his eyes. "Thank you."

"You're welcome. By the way…*you* look nice." Matt leaned over, breathing deeply. "And you smell nice too."

Trudy could feel the hairs on her neck standing up. How was he able to make her feel like this with just simple words and a look? She'd never had a man regard her the way Matt did. It was the look of a man who had been fasting for weeks and had been presented with his favorite meal.

Spinning around in her seat, hoping to alleviate some of her discomfort, she took a long sip of her margarita. "This is a nice hotel. Do you stay here often?"

"Actually, this is my first time, or else I might have known better than to have left you unattended at the bar."

Matt sent a glaring look over at the table Paul was sitting at, before returning his attention to Trudy. "So, what do you want to talk about?"

"What?" asked Trudy, confused.

"I messaged you saying we could meet for drinks if you ever wanted to talk, and now, you're here."

Trudy shook her head. "Oh, it was nothing. I just needed to get out of the house."

"Well, regardless. I am glad to see you aren't mad at me anymore."

"No, I'm not mad anymore," Trudy said, looking up from her drink, slowly shaking her head. "As you said, I knew how you felt about me, and I still kept meeting with you anyway."

Matt peered at her mischievously. "And yet, here you are, meeting me again."

Trudy took a moment, gathering the courage to respond. "Yes. I am," she said, looking brazenly into his eyes.

Matt arched one eyebrow. "Would you like to go somewhere… a little more private?"

Trudy gulped down the rest of her drink and placed the empty glass back on the bar. She then nodded her head. Matt took her hand, pulled her to her feet, and began guiding her to the elevators.

As they rode the elevator, Trudy trained her eyes on the numbers lighting up, as they marked their ascent. She was too anxious to look at Matt but could feel him staring at her.

She followed as he led her to his room and waited while he opened the door. Once the door closed behind them, he swept her into his arms and kissed her.

"Mm," he groaned against her lips. "What were you

drinking?"

Instead of answering him, Trudy leaned in further, deepening the kiss. She felt Matt's hands as they moved down her back, grabbing at her hips. She moaned as he drew her against him.

Placing her hands against his torso, she timidly ran them across his chest. He shivered beneath her touch, and she marveled at the realization that *she* could affect *him* in such a way.

Matt moved back just enough to loosen the belt from around her waist, sliding her dress off her shoulders and letting it fall to the floor. Trudy heard the sound of fabric ripping but ignored it.

A sigh escaped his lips as he stopped to admire her. "Has anyone ever told you how beautiful you are?" He lifted her up into his arms and carried her into the bedroom.

After laying her down on the bed, he began removing his clothes. Trudy watched in awe as parts of his body were revealed to her. She followed the length of his legs as he discarded his pants, purposely avoiding the girth between his legs. Her eyes trained on his chest as he unbuttoned his shirt. His build was lean and muscular, and her hands itched to touch him everywhere.

Trudy suddenly felt self-conscious and grabbed the covers, pulling them over her.

Once he was completely naked, Matt climbed into the bed beside her. "I have wanted you since the day I first saw you."

The day he first saw—Her thoughts were soon forgotten as Matt drew her closer, pulling her on top of him.

As his arms wrapped around her, crushing her body against his for another kiss, she felt his erection pressing against her abdomen, and she moved against it instinctively. A low guttural groan vibrated out against her lips.

"Slow down," he whispered. "I want to take things slow. If you do that again, I can't promise I'll be able to hold back."

"Sorry," she said, her voice thick with wanting. "I couldn't seem to help myself."

Matt searched her eyes, a curious look on his face. "What are you doing to me?"

Rolling over, he placed Trudy beneath him and began placing kisses along the length of her neck. His trail led him further down until he was hovering above her breast.

Opening his mouth, he blew out softly over her nipple, causing it to harden.

Trudy reached up, grabbed his head, and brought him closer. She could not stand the teasing. He was torturing her.

Matt shook his head. Instead of taking the nipple into his mouth, he flicked his tongue out sharply over the nub.

Trudy's whole body shivered in response.

As Matt continued the assault on her nipple, she placed her thumb against his tongue, reveling in the furor the two sensations stirred in her.

She could feel herself becoming wet and felt an emptiness inside her, as it throbbed in its need to be filled. She slid her hand down, grasping for him, but he swatted her hand away.

"Not yet," he said, his lips brushing against her nipple.

Reaching down between her legs, he placed two fingers inside of her. "Oh God, you're wet," he growled, the words thick with his desire.

"Please," said Trudy, a tiny whimper escaping her lips.

Matt locked onto her eyes. "You want me?"

"Yes," Trudy choked out.

Matt removed his fingers and drove deep inside her.

"Ah." *That's it*, she thought.

"Oh God. Trudy. Yes!" Matt exclaimed as he deepened his thrusts.

Trudy matched his movements, her arms wrapped around his lower back, bringing him forward, trying to pull him deeper. "Yes, Matt. Yes."

She followed the wave until every last ounce of her was satiated and spent. They were like two animals, their desires fierce and rutting, with one singular purpose: to fulfill an urge that could only be sated by the other.

Matt was as skillful a lover as she had believed he would be, and Trudy had enjoyed every single minute of it. But now that all the anger that had brought her here had dissipated, the repercussions of what she had done hit her full force, and the gravity of it all came crashing down.

Sitting up on the side of the bed, she felt tears rolling down her cheeks. She wiped her eyes, searching for her discarded clothes on top of the maroon carpet with gold geometric shapes.

Matt grabbed her arm, trying to pull her back into bed. "Where're you going? You don't have to leave so soon, do you? I thought we could take a… Are you crying?"

Trudy tried to hold back the tears, hoping they would wait until she made it into the bathroom, but Matt's concern only made her feel worse. The tears came pouring forth like a fountain.

Matt pulled her to him. "Was this your first time? Cheating?"

Trudy nodded her head against his shoulder.

"I'm sorry, this isn't how I wanted it to be. We should

have waited."

Trudy drew away and wiped her tears with the back of her hand. "I'm okay now." She lifted the corners of her mouth in an attempt at a smile. "I just need a shower. Do you mind?" she asked, pointing at the bathroom door.

"No, go ahead. It's yours."

Trudy scouted out her underwear and dress and hurried into the bathroom, closing the door behind her. She turned on the shower, sat down on the toilet, and cried.

She had believed that being with Matt would be some kind of magical answer to all her problems. How stupid could she be? All he had to do was show her a little attention, and she'd given in. Now, she was an adulterer. She felt even worse than she did before she came here.

"Well, crying and feeling sorry for yourself is not going to fix anything. The deed is done now. No sense in trying to put the adulterer back in the box," she chided herself aloud.

Trudy stepped into the shower, hoping to wash away some of the shame of what she'd done. But as hard as she scrubbed, it just wasn't going away.

Walking back into the room to look for her sandals, Trudy saw that Matt had already dressed and made the bed.

Good, she thought, *less evidence of the deed.*

Matt was waiting for her in the other room. He was sitting in one of the leather chaises. He wore a stern look on his face. "You want to talk?" he asked sympathetically.

"No, I think it's best that I go."

"If I had known—"

"Known what?" she snapped. "You would have what…treated me differently. Not pursued me?"

"No. Maybe. Trudy, you came here to *me*." Matt said, defending himself.

"I know," she said, sounding defeated. "I'm not blaming you. And no, I never cheated on my husband before."

For once, Matt seemed to be at a loss for words. Seeing that they both had nothing left to say, Trudy spied her sandals, grabbed her purse, and left.

Out in the hallway, she leaned against the wall as she waited for the elevator. Where to now? Where did people go after they cheated on their spouses? Did she go home and act as if nothing had happened, or did she come clean? She reached out and pressed the button for the elevator again. Too bad she didn't have enough money to hole up in one of these nice hotel rooms.

CHAPTER 5

"I T WAS ABOUT *this* big." Mr. Dalsin spread his hands out in front of him to demonstrate the size of the fish he'd caught with his son, while on their fishing trip this past weekend.

Trudy nodded her head and smiled, feigning interest. Although she was pleased that things between her and Mr. Dalsin were back to normal, she was hoping he would hurry up and finish his story so she could get back to work. What she was growing to believe was an overdramatized version of the real fish story, had gone on for at least ten minutes now, and she was becoming fearful that the conversation would eventually turn to her, and he'd want to hear her tale about what she'd been up to this weekend.

Getting any work done had already been a struggle. Every time she tried entering in a receipt from the sales made by the store over the weekend, thoughts of her visit to the hotel kept drifting in. Just being in the office, where Matt had been reintroduced to her just over a week ago, was challenging. She wondered what Mr. Dalsin would say if she were to share her "whopper" of a tale.

Thankfully, his assistant buzzed in, saying she needed Mr. Dalsin to look over some paperwork. Trudy silently thanked Peggy for saving her. Mr. Dalsin left, but reluctantly. He had just gotten to the part of the story where their boat had capsized.

Trudy still did not know how she had kept from

confessing her indiscretion to James. Luckily, he wasn't there when she returned home that day. Eric's had been the first face she'd seen when she walked in. After shedding tears at the hotel, she had remained calm the whole ride home, but had nearly broken down again when she saw Eric, thinking of how her impudence could have cost her, her entire family.

As soon as she walked in the door, Eric started going on about wanting to join some afterschool program.

"Have you talked it over with your father?" she'd asked.

"He told me to talk to you."

Of course, he had. It would be crazy to think that he would want to have an opinion when it came to his kids.

As she mulled over James's response, Eric pointed out a rip in the seam of her dress near her upper thigh. Trudy had nearly lost it. How had she gotten all the way home without noticing a tear of that size? She had quickly muted her expression, not wanting to reveal any guilt to her son. She'd thanked him for calling it to her attention and hurried off to the laundry room to find something to change into. Opting for sweatpants and a T-shirt out of the dryer. The dress had been shoved under a stack of dirty clothes.

Looking to avoid Eric, she remembered why she had come home early in the first place and ran upstairs to check on Cori, who appeared to be in better spirits, judging by her end of the conversation coming from the other side of her bedroom door. Trudy took that as a good sign and left Cori alone.

She then went to her bedroom and fell across the unmade bed. Just a few short hours ago, she had left that room, ready to commit an act that would forever mar her. She wished that she had known then, what she knew now, that she did not like the woman she would become.

True, she had been angry and hurt when she made her decision, and even now, she was still resentful towards James, but an affair was never the answer. Either you tried to work on your marriage, as she had tried to, or you ended it. James did not deserve what she'd done to him.

Three days later, Trudy was still weighing whether she should tell James or not, but after concluding that it was just a one-time thing and nothing like that would ever happen between her and Matt again—or any other man for that matter—she would keep her secret. But despite having made up her mind that Matt was off-limits, he had not come to the same conclusion. He had tried calling and leaving messages when she didn't answer. And texting her repeatedly, over and over again, for the last couple of days. Every message was an apology, asking her to call him.

Clearly, she was ignoring him, but he didn't seem to be getting the message. She had started leaving her phone on silent and checking it every half hour. If he didn't stop, she was going to have to block him.

Even with Mr. Dalsin out of the way, trying to get any work done at the office was proving to be futile. Trudy grabbed her purse and left. Hopefully, a bagel for lunch and a walk around the lake would help to clear her head.

She was unpleasantly surprised when Matt walked up behind her while standing in front of the register at the bagel shop.

He must not have liked the expression on her face when she turned around to confront him, because he immediately raised his hands out as if warding off some evil hex. "I didn't know what else to do. You haven't been responding to my messages."

Trudy paid for her meal and walked out of the bagel shop,

ignoring him. Matt followed behind. She stood in front of the store, assessing her current situation. Did she take the much-needed walk or run back to the office? Might as well stay where she was. She was pretty sure that regardless of whichever decision she made, Matt wasn't going anywhere, and she did not want to bring this back to work with her.

She headed off towards the lake with Matt by her side. He allowed her a few minutes to walk in silence before interrupting the lull. "Are you ever going to speak to me again?"

Chewing her bagel thoughtfully, she turned and looked up at him. "Why are we talking now?"

He started to reply but shook his head as if reconsidering. "After what happened, I think we should have *something* to say to each other."

"Are you on speaking terms with all your one-night stands?" Trudy bit out.

Matt stopped walking and stared at her incredulously.

Trudy wanted to keep walking, but it seemed inappropriate to leave him standing there, looking like a deer caught in the headlights. So, she stopped and waited.

"One-night stand?" He repeated. "I mean, I am not going to pretend that I have not had any during my lifetime, but…"

Trudy didn't know why, but it hurt to know she hadn't been the only one. Why should it matter to her who he had spent his time with? They barely knew each other. "…what we had was not, at least I did not plan for it to be, a one-night stand."

Trudy remembered his words to her that day. *I have wanted you since the day I first saw you.* "Matt, what do you want from me?"

"I told you. I wanted you from day one, and after having

had you, I want more." He started moving toward her.

Trudy raised her palm in front of her. "I'm married. Married with *two children*. What do you propose we do? Have an affair? I don't think I'm made for that sort of thing." She peered at him, hopeful. "Don't you have to get back to Texas soon?"

"Should have been back days ago." Matt smiled sheepishly, running his hand over his head. "Wish you'd come with me."

"Strange how you seem to have selective hearing sometimes. *The husband and kids*, what about them?"

"I don't know, Trudy. Really, I don't. Part of me knows that you have another life, but when I see you, I see you with me."

She had lost her appetite. Looking around for the nearest trash bin, Trudy walked over and tossed her unfinished bagel inside.

How did someone respond to such a declaration? She knew what she should say: yell at him and tell him he was crazy, that what they had done was a mistake, that he should forget about her and move on. But even now, with him so near, her mind was drawn back to that day, remembering what it felt like when he kissed her and touched her.

She felt Matt's arms wrapping around her from behind. Despite the day being warm, she felt herself shiver, and she leaned into the warmth of his embrace.

"Mm," Matt sighed, wrapping his arms tighter.

Trudy twisted around to face him.

"It's such a beautiful day. Isn't it?" said a woman passing by, speaking to her companion.

Trudy pushed against Matt's chest, wrenching away from him. What was the matter with her? Had she lost her mind?

Allowing a man who was not her husband to hold her like that in public. What if someone she knew had seen them?

A voice in the back of her mind reminded her, *James had never been one for public shows of affection. Hadn't it, just for a moment, felt nice to be with someone who chased caution to the wind? Who didn't care if people saw you?* She pushed the thought away. None of that mattered.

"Are you going to pretend you didn't feel that?" asked Matt, breaking through her thoughts.

"Are *you* going to pretend that it's not appropriate?" Trudy tossed back at him. "Don't you understand? We can't do this."

Matt appeared to have given up, at least for the day. He drew his hands up and then let them fall back down to his sides. "You know what? You're right. I need to consider your feelings in all of this and give you some space. I'll let you get back to your day." Matt turned to walk away but then glanced back over his shoulder. "But I'll be back."

"Stupid woman," Trudy scolded herself. *You thought sleeping with Matt would somehow solve all your problems. Now, things are even worse.* But even as he walked away, part of her ached to call him back.

It was opening night at the fair, and it seemed as though everyone in town was there. Trudy had pleaded with Cori to put off going until Sunday when it would likely be less crowded. But Cori had ignored her reasoning, questioning why anyone would want to go to the fair when no one else was there, and adding, that she could just go with Tara if no one else wanted to come.

Going to the fair each spring had been a family tradition

since the kids were little, and regardless of the state of her marriage, Trudy was not ready to end the tradition yet. Besides, it wasn't just her; Eric had wanted to come as well, and James had insisted that going on a Saturday was no big deal, even though Trudy was sure he'd barely had any sleep and would have preferred to go on Sunday as well. He also hated crowds, even more than she did, often complaining about how claustrophobic it made him feel and griping anytime the foot traffic became stagnated.

They had ended up bringing Tara with them anyway, and both girls had quickly disappeared right after she'd given Cori money. Trudy had tried giving her a twenty-dollar bill, but Cori had just stood there with her hand out, looking at her mother as if she were a simpleton until Trudy conceded and relinquished another twenty.

Trudy had yelled after them to meet back there in two hours, but she doubted the two girls had heard her.

Even with funds being tight, she still managed to put aside money for the fair each year. Usually, she paid for the kids and their friends, but thankfully, Tara was able to pay her own way this time. Eric had been given the option to invite a friend as well but decided it would be more fun to hang out with Trudy and James.

Although she suspected it was Eric's way of trying to rectify the distance between her and James, Trudy was grateful for the buffer. Things between her and James had been awkward for the last week, and she had avoided being alone with him whenever possible.

They stopped at the ticket booth to buy wristbands for both James and Eric, which would allow them entrance onto all the rides. Trudy was not a big fan of sitting in a mechanical contraption that was taken apart several times a year, as the people who owned it traveled from one town to the other. She came to the fair strictly as an observer. She would, however, love to ride the helicopter. She planned on it every year, but there never seemed to be enough money left over after doling it out to everyone else.

As soon as they were handed their wristbands, both Ericand James headed straight to the bumper cars, as they had every year since Eric was big enough. Trudy trailed behind, glancing around at the other patrons.

As the sun set, the lights at the fair turned on in an inherent reaction. The colors of the horizon seemed to want to join in, but the gaudiness produced by the fluorescent lights was in cruel contrast to the many brilliant shades painted by the skyline.

There were booths set up everywhere. At one stand, a man was trying to win his daughter a goldfish by tossing a white ball into a vase filled with water. At another, people were whacking away at moles vying for stuffed animals. A giant giraffe hung from the top of the stand, tempting passersby. Trudy spied Cori, Tara, and what appeared to be a few students from their school, shooting water at a target, trying to get their yellow ducks to swim faster than the others.

She remembered when she and James used to come to the fair when they were dating. Back then, she was naïve about the rides and the dangers they presented and only craved the thrill of being packed in close quarters with 'her man' as she yelled and was tossed around with only him there to save her. They would wander around inside the house of mirrors, stopping off in corners in hopes of making out. Back then, they couldn't keep their hands off each other. Back then, James loved trying to show off for her at the booths in hopes of winning her the biggest prize. The shooting gallery was his favorite.

Trudy scanned the group of people on the bumper cars, looking for her family, and saw that James had been staring at her, right before Eric rammed his car into his. There had been a wistful look in his eyes, and she wondered if he had been thinking of those times as well.

A few minutes later, the ride ended, and the two of them made their way to the exit. Eric's face was lit up with excitement. "We should do that again. Dad was like a sitting target."

Trudy searched James's face for a reaction; she wondered how long he had been staring at her. Had he sensed the distance between them lately as well? "He's probably not on his game," she quipped. "You know he's missing out on sleep for this."

A pained expression flitted across James's face.

Trudy wished she could take it back. She had meant no harm, but James spending more time in bed than with her or the kids, had been a long-standing argument between the two of them.

"Don't worry. When you guys get to the ring toss, he'll show you who's boss." She smiled at James, but he had closed off his expressions to her.

"That's right. Let's see how much junk you're talking after I beat you at one of these booths." James said, teasing Eric.

"Can I get something to eat first?" Eric asked.

"Sure, lead the way," Trudy responded.

They followed behind Eric as he sought out a food vendor that sold hotdogs.

Trudy could feel James staring at her again. "Are you happy?" he asked.

The question threw her, and it took her a minute to answer. "What makes you ask that?"

"I don't know. I was thinking back to when we were younger. Before the kids, when it was just us, and how you used to smile all the time. I can't remember the last time I saw you smile."

Trudy didn't know what to say. She had been trying to get James to notice her for so long, to see that she was unhappy, and *now* he had. If he had noticed before she—. Fortunately, she didn't have to answer. Eric had settled on a corn dog vendor, and while they waited in line, he grabbed James's attention, wanting to know what the two of them would ride next.

While the two males in her life were trying to determine in which order they would tackle each ride, Trudy considered what her answer would be to James if he were to revisit the question. It was hard for James to talk about emotional matters, and Trudy knew it took a lot for him to have asked her about her feelings in the first place.

Maybe a simple answer of 'no' would suffice. If Trudy got into all the reasons why she wasn't happy, that would just start another argument. Then again, maybe it was best to leave it alone. Tonight was supposed to be about fun, so she would do her best to keep it that way.

"You sure you want to eat before you go on any of those rides?" Trudy asked, her question directed at Eric. "You know what happened last time."

"Mom," whined Eric. "You know that only happened once. Years ago."

"If you say so." Trudy rolled her eyes, smirking.

Eric shot her a look as if contemplating a response but then rolled his eyes instead, deciding against it.

Within a few hours, Trudy was tired and just about ready to go. Even Cori and Tara, who had found Trudy first, were asking when they could leave and where the boys were.

Eric and James were just stepping off their last ride, and after spotting them, made their way over to Trudy and the girls. Everyone began chatting excitedly, comparing their experiences on the rides with each other.

Trudy was glad that everyone had enjoyed themselves. It was a rare occasion when no one found anything to complain about. She was just about to get in line for the helicopter ride when the girls had spotted her, but no matter; she could use the extra money to fill the tank.

It had taken them forever to get home from the fair. The line of cars had stretched back to the end of the parking lot, and nearly no one was willing to let anyone in front of them. By the time they'd left the fairgrounds and dropped off Tara, the car was down to a quarter tank of gas.

Trudy made a pit stop at a nearby gas station while ignoring James, as he tried to convince her there was enough gas to get them home. A low dial always made Trudy nervous. James, on the other hand, would drive home from work with the needle on 'E.'

The house was shrouded in darkness when they pulled into the driveway. No one had remembered to turn the lights on before they left. As they entered the house, Blue could be heard moving around in his cage, anxiously waiting to be let out.

The kids came in, flipping light switches in their wake as if making up for the electricity they had saved earlier. Trudy was walking towards Blue when Eric stepped ahead of her.

"I got 'em, Mom."

Trudy stopped, smiling at her son. Eric could surprise her sometimes.

Instead of heading to bed, Trudy put on a pot of water for tea, thinking it would allow James and her an opportunity to finish their conversation from earlier. "Anyone else want tea?"

James mumbled something about being tired and headed upstairs, barely looking in her direction.

Oh well, thought Trudy, taking the boiling water off the stove. Maybe she would watch something on TV. There was bound to be an old movie on.

Sitting down in front of the TV, Trudy grabbed the remote and started scrolling through the channels until she landed on an old black-and-white movie. She then picked up her phone and turned it back on. It had been off since she'd gotten home from work, making sure she avoided any unwanted calls. As soon as the phone powered on, she saw that she had a voicemail and several text messages. She'd check the text first. She was sure the voicemail was from Matt, and she was not prepared to hear whatever he had to say. The deep, hushed timber of his tone had a way of sending shivers running straight right through her.

A few of the texts were from companies advertising weekend sales, and one from Matt saying, 'Sorry, please call me.'

Not so bad. If the voicemail was from him, it was probably much more of the same thing.

She took a chance and played it and she was wrong.

It was Matt, but his voice on the message was deeper and held the hint of a slur. It sounded as if he'd been drinking. He was saying that he missed her and couldn't get her off his mind. He then began to describe, in vivid detail, some of the things he would do to Trudy if he had her there with him right now.

How he would strip her naked. The many places he wanted to put his tongue. How he wanted to suck and taste her until she came fast and hard. Then how he would fu—

She knew she should cut the message short and delete it, especially with her husband right upstairs, but she couldn't seem to stop herself from listening. She could picture Matt doing everything he was describing to her, and she ached to feel his touch on her again. She listened to the message once more before putting the phone down and tried to distract herself with the movie on the television set. Unfortunately, the man in the film was just sweeping a woman into his arms before planting her with a passionate kiss. At first, the woman struggled, trying to fight him off, but in the end, she relinquished, wrapping her arms around his neck, and gave in.

Trudy turned the TV off, tossed the remote on the table, and went upstairs.

A thick, dark mass of clouds covered the afternoon sky. It had been raining off and on since Trudy woke up that morning. As she listened to the rain in its attempt to lull her back to sleep, she yearned for just one day to stay in bed and take refuge under the covers, but such was not the life she led.

After finally forcing herself out of bed, she had a bright idea and called Shawna to see if she was free for brunch, and for once, not only had her answer been yes, but she had actually shown up.

While waiting for the waiter to return with their food, they observed the other diners and made small talk about the weather. The day wasn't the only thing that was overcast; it felt like a dark cloud was hanging over the two of them.

Shawna was her oldest friend, well, her only friend, and Trudy did not like having this rift between them. "Hey," she said, reaching across the table to grab Shawna's hand. "How've things been since we last talked?"

Shawna flinched as if remembering something unpleasant, but quickly shook it off as only Shawna could. "Great, still enjoying my free time. Greg will be back in a few days, though."

"Bet you can't wait." Trudy joked.

Suddenly, Shawna's mood shifted, and she became sullen. "I'm thinking about leaving him."

"Okay," said Trudy, drawing out the word. She loved her friend dearly and would be there for her, no matter what. But she did not want to say the wrong thing in case Shawna changed her mind.

"But I'm scared. I've never been on my own, and I don't know what I would do without him."

Trudy hated seeing her friend like this, but she wasn't sure what she should say or do. She'd offer to let Shawna come and stay with her, but she wasn't sure how she or James would react once Greg showed up demanding that his wife come back home. And knowing Shawna the way she did, she would most likely see the offer as some sort of handout and have too much pride to accept it for what it was anyway: one friend looking out for the other.

"I'm no expert, but I am sure there are programs that can help you make the transition. That's if you've decided that's what you want." Trudy added.

Trudy spied the waiter coming towards them with their food. By the time their food was placed in front of them and the waiter was gone, Shawna's mood had changed again.

"So, how's things at home with you? You still got the hots for that ex-coworker?"

Trudy was thrown by Shawna's question, but she would let it pass. Shawna obviously needed the distraction from her own life, and Trudy had been trying to figure out how to bring Matt up anyway.

"Yeah, about that." Trudy looked down, avoiding eye contact.

"Giirrrl, no, you didn't?" Shawna said a little too loudly, drawing looks from the people at the nearby tables.

"Shh," Trudy chided. "I don't want everyone to know."

"Please, you don't know these people," Shawna responded but lowered her voice. "When did this happen?"

"One day last week."

"So?"

"So what?" Trudy asked.

"How was it?" Shawna twisted in her seat as she crossed her arms in front of her.

"I tell you I cheated on my husband, and you want juicy details."

Shawna lifted her eyebrow and scrunched her lips. "This surprises you. Why?"

She was right. What had Trudy expected? Condolences? For Shawna to ask her how she felt? No, that was *her* role in their friendship.

Trudy speared a forkful of salad and shoved it into her mouth. "It was good." She nodded as she mumbled the words out over her mouthful.

"Mm-hmm. Is that all? Just good? So, you invited me out

to tell me you cheated on your husband, and now you feel bad because it wasn't even worth it?" Shawna sat waiting for an answer.

Trudy took a sip from her water, sat it back on the table, and tapped her fingers against the glass for several seconds.

"What do you want to hear, that it was probably *the best sex I've ever had in my life*? That *now*, while I hate myself, I *still want him*?" Trudy gazed around at the eyes staring back at her, realizing she had been yelling.

"Well, no. It's not what *I* wanted to hear." Shawna looked around, laughing. "But evidently, it's what you needed to say."

"I just think it wouldn't be so bad if he just let it end with that one time and went back to Texas. But he keeps messaging, telling me he wants more."

"Yeah, I can see how that can be a problem. But what do *you* want?" Shawna asked.

"Honestly, I don't know what I want anymore, or if I ever did. I thought I wanted my marriage, my family, but I am tired of trying to get my husband to open up to me, and fight for us. But I also can't see me jeopardizing the little bit that I do have, for a man I barely know, who lives in a whole other state."

"Why not just see him when he comes into town? Kind of like I do when Greg leaves?"

Trudy didn't like that Shawna was comparing her life to hers, but then again, what did it matter if it was one man or five? Infidelity was infidelity.

"I don't know. I haven't gotten past the first time to think of doing it on a regular basis."

Okay, enough about that. Trudy didn't come here to talk about their problems at home. She was here to share a meal nd spend time with her friend.

"Share some of that." Trudy leaned across the table with her fork, ready to sample some of the food from Shawna's plate.

Shawna swatted her fork away teasingly. "I haven't eaten all day. You might want to be careful. I might end up eating what's on *my* plate and yours."

Trudy looked at her friend affectionately and smiled. She was glad that the tension between them had passed. "You know, I'll always be here if you need me?"

Shawna looked at Trudy, a haunting expression in her eyes. "I know, Trudy. I know."

CHAPTER 6

RUNNING TO THE door, she stumbled over a crack in the sidewalk but caught herself before falling to the pavement beneath her. She climbed the steps up the porch. When she reached the front door, she began to bang her fist against it repeatedly, calling out, "Shawna! Shawna! Let Me In! Shawna!"

Trudy had been busy working from home earlier when she noticed a missed call and message from Shawna. She had tried calling her back several times, but the phone continued to ring unanswered before sending her to voicemail. When she checked the message, Trudy had been instantly on alert. Shawna's words had been slurred, saying how much she loved Trudy, missed their closeness, and how sorry she was that she had to leave her.

Now, her friend wasn't answering the door. She grabbed the doorknob, turned, and it gave way in her hand. The first thing she noticed when she walked in, was dead silence—it was too quiet. But she remembered seeing Shawna's car in the driveway. She'd barely missed it when she pulled in—so she searched the first floor of the house. Confident that no one was there, she ran upstairs to check the rooms above.

Once she reached the top of the landing, she realized she had never been upstairs and had no idea where to find Shawna's bedroom.

From the end of the hallway, she heard moaning and stilled herself to listen, hoping it would help her determine where the sounds were coming from. What seemed like an hour, but most likely only a minute, passed before she heard it again. "Shawna!" She yelled as she ran.

She barreled into a bedroom at the end of the hall. Clothes were strewn all over the floor and the bed. Turning to her right, Trudy walked cautiously into the bathroom, where she found Shawna lying across the linoleum floor, her hand gripped around an empty bottle of pills.

Trudy flew to Shawna, struggling to pull her into her arms. Her body was limp and unyielding.

"Shawna. Can you hear me!?" Trudy patted her hand repeatedly against Shawna's cheek. "What did you take?"

Shawna's eyes fluttered open and appeared unfocused as she tried to make out the figure in front of her. "Trudy…you? Let me sleep," she slurred.

Instinctively, Trudy pulled Shawna over to the toilet, placed two fingers in her mouth, and shoved them down her throat. Shawna's hands struck out defensively, trying to swat Trudy away whilst her body convulsed against the intrusion.

She retched and grabbed hold of the toilet, just as a mixture of bile and pills flowed freely into the bowl.

Trudy fell against the vanity, with one hand still pressed against Shawna's back, relieved. Beneath her palm, she could feel Shawna's body shaking, this time as she lay on top of the toilet seat, sobbing.

Although her worst fears had passed, Trudy knew it wasn't over. Her friend needed help. Help she could not give her. She reached for the phone in her back pocket and called 911.

Trudy was still sitting on the bathroom floor when she heard the sirens approaching. Reaching over, she swept the hair back from Shawna's face as if somehow, despite her pasty skin and sweat-soaked hair, this simple gesture would make her look more presentable. "It's okay. You're going to get some help now."

"Okay," said Shawna, curling into a ball and closing her eyes.

Trudy was just about to shake her, worried that some of the pills were still in her system and starting to take effect, when she heard the paramedics running up the stairs. "Back here," she shouted.

Before she knew it, Shawna had been hoisted up and placed on a stretcher, and she was being questioned by the paramedics. What time had she found Shawna, and what had she taken? It had all suddenly become too much, and now that she was coming down from her adrenaline rush, all Trudy could do was muster up enough strength to hand off the empty bottle, and point toward the toilet where the pills were still floating inside.

How many times had she reread that same exact sentence? Trudy gave up and tossed the magazine she was holding back onto the table. It was getting really hard to concentrate on anything while sitting around waiting for an update on Shawna's condition. The freezing temperatures in the hospital didn't make it any easier. And each time someone walked into the waiting room, she became anxious thinking it might be one of Shawna's doctors with some news.

Trudy picked up her coffee, hoping the heat from the cup would abate some of the chill. Sadly, the coffee had become tepid as it sat untouched. She felt lonely and vulnerable sitting in the waiting room by herself. Glancing around, she saw families gathered in small groups, there to offer support to each other, while she sat there alone. She had tried calling James, but he'd been too busy installing a new heating and cooling system in a customer's home.

She had thought about going to get Cori from school. If any other person cared about what had happened to Shawna, it was her daughter. But it was her senior year, and Cori shouldn't have to deal with something of this magnitude. Besides, Trudy couldn't leave the hospital without hearing something first.

Not knowing who else to call, she finally settled on Matt. He had barely answered the phone before she began apologizing for ignoring his calls. Trudy explained that she was following an ambulance to the hospital with her friend inside and asked if he could come.

He had not hesitated, asked what hospital, and said he was on his way.

She was refreshing her cup of coffee when she saw movement out of the corner of her eye. Looking up, expecting to see a doctor, she was pleased to see it was Matt instead, searching the room for her. Trudy hesitated long enough to place her cup on the counter and ran to him, allowing him to pull her into his embrace.

As Matt loosened his grip to back away, Trudy clung to him a little longer, not ready to let go. But once the tension she had been feeling was gone, she let go and looked up at

Matt self-consciously. "Sorry about that."

"No problem. Whatever I can do to help. That's what I'm here for." He smiled.

Trudy walked over to the seat she had been occupying before Matt arrived. Instead of slouching over as she had been before, she sat up a little straighter now that she was not alone.

"Has there been any word?" asked Matt, sitting down beside her.

"No. Not since I got here. At first, they were not even going to talk to me at all, saying we're not related, but Shawna was able to give her consent."

"I'm sure she's going to be alright. It seems you got to her in time."

"Yeah, physically." The stress of the day had started to creep back in, along with the uncertainty of Shawna doing something like this again. "But what about mentally?"

"Well," said Matt, leaning over and patting her hand. "That's for the doctors to worry about, not you."

"Easy for you to say," she snapped.

Trudy knew Matt was trying to help, but how was she not supposed to worry? It wasn't like there was a switch she could turn off.

They both sat in silence while Trudy resumed flipping through the magazine, and Matt checked emails on his phone.

A few minutes later, a doctor walked in, wearing green scrubs with a surgical mask hanging from his pocket, looking for the members of the Hall family.

Trudy rushed over. "Here."

The doctor explained that Shawna was in stable condition and commended Trudy on her quick thinking, in helping to expel the pills from her system. He said Trudy may have saved her life. Currently, they were waiting on a room to open up in the psychiatric ward and still trying to contact Shawna's husband.

The doctor looked mindfully at Trudy. "You did good. Your friend's going to be okay. Go home and get some rest now." He nodded at Matt and left.

Trudy walked back to her chair and sat down, resigning herself to staying at the hospital and keeping watch.

Matt stood up and leaned down until he was eye-to-eye with her. "Trudy. Time to go."

Trudy met his eyes, thinking to challenge him, but there was no contention left in her. She was tired of fighting. She gave in and allowed him to lead her out of the hospital. Several minutes had passed before she realized she was in Matt's car headed down the highway.

"Where are we going?"

Matt stole a glance over at her. "You've had a pressing day. Let me take care of you."

Trudy didn't know where this was headed, but she was too tired to care. She sat back in her seat and focused on the cars zipping in and out of the lanes ahead of her.

Before long, they were pulling into the parking lot outside Matt's hotel. As they entered the lobby, Trudy followed behind docilely, up the elevator to his room.

Once the door closed behind them, Trudy felt as if a barrier within her chest had broken loose, and she fell to the floor, grabbing her knees to her, and rocked as waves of emotions swept through her. She wailed as tears flowed from her eyes.

As she wept, she felt strong arms wrap around her. Part of her wanted to fight against the solace that the embrace provided, so that she could give in to the despair and drown in it. Another, stronger part, leaned in and accepted the support that she was due.

Matt pulled back to look down at her and began wiping the tears from her eyes. "You feel better now?"

Trudy sniffled and smiled self-consciously. "I think so." What was it about Matt that allowed her to show her vulnerable side? A side she kept hidden from most people, even herself.

"Good." He got up from the floor, walked over to a small bar, and poured dark liquid into a glass. He held it up, offering it to Trudy.

She shook her head, remembering the last time they were together in his hotel room. The memory caused her cheeks to flush, and she quickly looked away to hide her unease.

As if sensing her thoughts. "Sorry, I probably shouldn't have brought you back here, but I couldn't think of any other place," said Matt.

"It's okay," said Trudy, getting up from the floor and sitting down in one of the chairs. "As much as I wanted to be at the hospital, I needed to get away."

Matt sat down in a chair beside her.

"I just can't believe she was in so much pain that she wanted to try and…Why couldn't she talk to me?"

Matt shrugged his shoulders. "Maybe she didn't want to worry you." He reached over, drew Trudy out of her chair, sat her on his lap, and held her.

They sat that way for a while. Both lost in their own thoughts until Trudy noticed a part of Matt poking into her thigh. The idea of his erection growing, knowing that he wanted her, caused her to grow warm.

She had fought her desire for him this past week, ignoring his calls and messages, but at this moment, she needed to escape to a place of pleasure, where sorrow and uncertainty did not exist.

Trudy twisted around on Matt's lap, angling herself in front of him, and placed her lips on top of his. At first, the kiss was tentative but soon grew deeper as Matt crushed her to him. She parted her lips, and he thrust his tongue inside. The invasion elicited an electrical pulse that ran to the nips of her toes.

Needing to feel closer to him, she wiggled around, careful not to break contact, and straddled her legs around his hips.

Matt moved his hands down her back, grabbing at her waist, and began grinding into her. She moaned against his lips, grinding back to answer him.

He pulled away, breathless. "Are you sure about this?"

Trudy stood up, kicked off her shoes, and began removing her clothes.

Seeing her response, Matt stood up and did the same. When he turned to walk towards the bedroom, Trudy pulled him back. He looked at her, confused, until he saw her staring pointedly at the chair and sat back down. Trudy stopped for a second to ogle his naked body before climbing back on his lap and lowering herself on top of him.

She wrapped her arms around his neck, pulling him to her, still needing the solace he provided. In a fevered frenzy, she rode him, his erection filling her, as she ground into him, seeking her release until she could feel it mounting. When it came, she fell against him, spent. The stress built up within her, immediately expelled.

Trudy was shaken from her respite by the ringing of her phone, causing her to jump up in alarm. Her phone was lying on a nearby table, and she saw that it was James calling.

"Hello," she answered, trying to sound at ease.

"Hey, I was calling to see if you were doing okay, and if you still needed me to come by the hospital."

"No, no," said Trudy, stuttering. "Actually, I was just about to leave." She felt a knot forming in her gut at the lie.

"Well, okay. I'll just head back to the office and finish up the paperwork. Then stop and pick something up on my way home. I know you're probably too worried to cook anything. Is there anything you want in particular?"

"Whatever you want is fine," she responded hurriedly. It seemed wrong to continue a conversation with her husband with Matt present.

He must have felt the same, because he grabbed a few items of clothing from a bureau and went into the bathroom.

"How's Shawna? Everything okay? You seem distracted."

"Yes, everything is okay. I mean…" Trudy stopped, catching herself. "No, it's not okay. They're going to keep her for a while for observation, and she'll be under psychiatric care."

"Makes sense. Sorry about your friend. I guess I'll see you when I get home?"

"Okay. See you then. Bye." Trudy ended the call.

She waited for the twinge of guilt that she knew would come, but for some reason, it did not. Even the knot from the lie she had told had already subsided. Perhaps it was only because she was still distraught over Shawna.

She should leave. There was still work that needed her attention, and it would not be long before the kids and James were home, but she also needed to clean up before leaving. She wondered if Matt would mind some company.

Despite it being 6:30 in the morning, the sun had yet to show its face as Trudy sat at the kitchen island, sipping her second cup of coffee, hoping it would wake her. Ever since the incident with Shawna, she had lain awake most nights, tossing and turning, only getting around maybe five hours of sleep. Last night had not been any different.

Too bad she could not be more like James, who didn't seem to let anything trouble him and could sleep through a thunderstorm.

It had also not helped that Cori had been treating her as if she was somehow responsible for Shawna's suicide attempt. After Trudy had sat down both the kids to tell them what happened, Cori had begun treating her even less cordially than usual, walking out every time Trudy entered a room. Even still, she had tried getting Cori to talk to her, thinking the change in behavior may have been due to how hard she was taking the news, but Cori had simply rolled her eyes, responding with an emphatic, "Nothing's wrong, Mom."

Another thing keeping her up at night was her thoughts about Matt. She was constantly daydreaming about their time together. It worried her that fantasizing about him was no longer accompanied by any of her usual guilt. Now, when he called, if she was alone, she answered. If she wasn't alone, she texted him the number 412, the anniversary of the first time they had been together, to let him know she was thinking of him.

Morally, she knew it was wrong, but mentally and physically, she craved the attention. The walls she had put up against him had been torn down as soon as he had shown up for her that day at the hospital. But what that meant for their future, she did not know.

Blue began stirring in his cage. He did a full circle before sitting back down and staring at her. Trudy supposed she should take him out before waking Eric. The morning air could maybe help do what the coffee could not. Before going into work today, she planned to try and visit Shawna *again*. Now that Greg was back in town, the hospital staff was refusing to let Trudy see her.

As Trudy and Blue made their way quietly down the sidewalk, she noticed how the whole neighborhood appeared to still be at rest, except for a dotting of houses here and there, where the lights were on in the bathroom or kitchen windows. Dew clung to the grass as it waited, like her and the rest of the world, to begin the day anew.

With Shawna in the hospital, Greg banning her from visiting, and things slow at work, Trudy wished she had enough money to take a short vacation—just a couple of days to help her get some perspective on the new life she had stepped into, a few short weeks ago.

There *was* an old college friend she had reconnected with on social media a few months back who had been begging her to visit, and Beverly only lived a little over a hundred miles away. Trudy had been putting her off, telling her that she did not have the time when really it was because she was ashamed of her lack of success. Keeping the books at a local hardware store barely compared to some of the careers her other alumni had entered into after graduating college. Beverly was the head of the financial department for a major company.

She was probably just being silly, making a big deal out of nothing. They had been pretty good friends in college, and Trudy was sure they could find more to talk about besides their careers. Both were married with teenage daughters. That alone should be enough to keep them busy for months. She would talk it over with James, and if he okayed it, she would let Beverly know of her plans to visit and then see if she could take the time off from work.

CHAPTER 7

THE TRIP TO Beverly's house had not taken long. The GPS marked the time at an hour and twenty minutes, but the time spent in the car watching as the countryside passed by, had been therapeutic for Trudy. She'd packed a few snacks before leaving home, so there would not be any reason to stop along the way. Although, a few billboards advertising antique shops had piqued her interest and almost tempted her to veer off the highway.

It had been easy to plan this mini vacation. When she'd asked for the time off from work, Mr. Dalsin had regarded her for several seconds as if he were looking at a stranger before finally responding. "I didn't think you believed in taking vacations. But of course, the time is there for you to use it. Enjoy yourself."

At first, she had been confused by his reaction before it dawned on her that it had been five years since her last vacation.

Everyone at home had basically shown indifference to her leaving for a few days. James only questioned how much money it would cost. Cori was still treating her as if she was responsible for all that was wrong with the world, and could care less if Trudy was there or not. The only person who'd shown any interest was Eric. He'd said he would miss her but understood she needed some time to herself.

Trudy's main concern had been for Blue. Luckily, his Vet's kennel had space for him over the weekend, and she received a discount for being a loyal customer. She did not trust James or the kids to be responsible enough to watch him while she was gone.

Trudy had left right after she had woken up Eric for school, making sure they had breakfast and hugging both kids goodbye. Cori had remained stoic during the exchange but did not push her away.

Beverly lived in a very affluent neighborhood. Huge maple trees and manicured hedges lined every street, and no house was less than 4,500 square feet. Trudy passed by several women pushing strollers, with toddlers tagging along behind them, as she drove by.

"You have reached your destination.," announced the voice navigation as she pulled up to a house at the end of a cul-de-sac. The one-story home was styled in the fashion of 18th-century French architecture. A cobblestone path led to an outdoor seating area that could be seen when looking out of the picture window at the front of the house. It was adjacent to the front door, which was situated inside of an archway.

Trudy was immediately aware of the same self-consciousness that had kept her from becoming reacquainted with her college friend in the first place. She hastily chided herself. *Material things were just that*. Beverly was a person outside her possessions.

The front door began to open as Trudy strode toward it. On the other side of the doorway stood Beverly, beaming, little crinkles forming near her eyes. She held her arms outstretched in front of her, expectantly. Trudy had forgotten she was a hugger.

It was like the years had never passed. Before her was an old college friend, whom the years had been very good to. She and Trudy were about the same height. But where Trudy still had a slight bulge from giving birth to Eric, Beverly was as flat as a pancake. Everything about her appeared perfectly trimmed, like someone who was a frequent customer of the salon.

Trudy dropped the overnight bag she'd been carrying and stepped into Beverly's hug.

"I've missed you so much," said Beverly. "It's been too long."

"It sure has."

After placing her things in the guestroom, Beverly gave Trudy a tour of the house.

The spacious kitchen featured a mosaic backsplash, stainless steel appliances, a walk-in pantry, and an informal dining spot. A sliding door led to a screened-in porch with a view of the backyard. They made their way to the master bedroom, which was almost twice the size of Trudy's, before returning to the living room, where a platter of cheese, crackers, and other delicacies were laid out on the coffee table.

Trudy sat on the sofa while Beverly headed into the kitchen, returning with a bottle of Moscato and two glasses. Beverly twisted off the bottle top and began to pour two hefty glasses of wine. "We have the house to ourselves this weekend. The kids are with their dad."

"Some sort of vacation?" asked Trudy, leaning over to take her glass.

"Oh, no. I guess I forgot to mention that David and I are separated. We're getting a divorce." Beverly delivered the news like she was talking about the weather.

"I'm sorry to hear that," Trudy responded apologetically.

"Nothing to be sorry for. It was long overdue. I mean, it was good for a while," Beverly said, staring off wistfully. "But we kind of grew apart and began taking each other for granted. Eventually, I found out that David was having an affair."

"You must have been devastated."

"You would have thought so, but no, I was actually relieved. It gave me an out I'd been looking for. But, don't get me wrong, I didn't let him off that easy, even though it was for the best. Now I get this beautiful home to myself every other weekend."

Trudy wondered how gracious James would be if he found out about her and Matt. What would *she* have to give up if he did?

"You okay over there?" questioned Beverly. "You seem to have gone off somewhere. How are things with you at home?"

Normally, Trudy wouldn't have been so open to sharing her business, but even though it had been years since they'd talked, Beverly was no stranger. In fact, in college, there weren't too many things about themselves that they hadn't shared with the other.

"Not so great. James and I mostly fight. But then again, not so much lately." Trudy looked off thoughtfully. "We've come to a point where we barely communicate."

Beverly chuckled a little to herself. "Ah, I remember those days. It's like two strangers sharing the same home."

"Precisely." Trudy agreed.

Both women looked at each other and laughed.

"So, do you have any extracurricular activities?" asked Beverly before taking a sip of wine.

It was an innocent enough question, but it struck a chord in Trudy.

"How do you mean?" she asked cautiously.

"You know, like yoga or a book club. Something to fill your time. Something for you."

"No," Trudy shook her head. "Nothing like that. It's mostly home and work."

"Mostly, huh?" Beverly raised one eyebrow and waited for an answer. When she saw that Trudy was not going to take the bait, she changed the subject. "How about a decent lunch? These snacks aren't going to cut it."

Trudy smiled, thankful that her friend had not tried to push her to talk, something Shawna would not have been so quick to do. "That sounds good. Mind if I freshen up in my room first?"

Beverly headed into the kitchen, allowing Trudy to find her way back to her room.

Thankfully, the guestroom had its own bath. She took a quick wash-up after changing out of her travel clothes.

By the time Trudy made her way back towards the kitchen, Beverly had set the table. It was a simple fair that consisted of a small vegetable salad with vinaigrette dressing and half a grilled panini sandwich. The two wine glasses had been transported over as well.

"I hope turkey and cheese is okay?"

"Yes," replied Trudy. "And even if it were not, I would not complain. I can't remember the last time someone prepared a meal for me that wasn't from a restaurant. Thank you."

"No problem. Gives me something to do with the kids out of the house."

Trudy had assumed Beverly had a busy schedule to fill her time and had put it on hold for her this weekend. Maybe being the head of the financial department had its perks.

"So, what extracurricular activities do *you* have to fill *your* time?" asked Trudy, repeating back Beverly's question to her earlier, as she took a seat at the table.

Beverly smiled, realizing what she was doing. "To be honest, other than a few yoga classes each week and tidying up around here, not much. I took some time off from work after the separation to help the kids with the transition—at least that's what I told myself anyway—but other than that, not much."

"Have you considered dating?" Trudy took a bite of her sandwich.

One would have thought Trudy had suddenly grown two heads from the look Beverly gave her. "Dating. At our age?"

"It's not unheard of, you know. I know it was while you two were still married, but even David was able to find someone."

"Yeah, but he's a man. It's easier for them," acknowledged Beverly.

Despite Beverly's assurance that she was okay with the separation, it could not have helped her friend's confidence to have her husband leave her for another woman.

"I don't know if anyone has told you lately," said Trudy, giving Beverly an appraising look, "But you look pretty good for your age."

Beverly placed the fork she was holding down beside her plate, clasped her hands together, and responded cantingly. "Why, Trudy, you say the nicest things."

Trudy knew it was Beverly's way of trying to soften the increasingly serious conversation, but she also questioned how long *had it been* since someone complimented her. One of the main reasons she had fallen for Matt was because of how special he made her feel. Trudy was a testament to how powerful a simple word of endearment could be. It also hadn't hurt to have it come from someone so enticingly seductive.

"But seriously, Beverly, you're still an attractive woman. I know it wouldn't be hard for you to find a man to share your time with."

"Well, I'm not so sure I'm ready for a relationship right now."

"Who said anything about a relationship? When I said, 'share your time,'" Trudy emphasized using air quotes. "I meant along the lines of getting laid."

Beverly nodded her head slowly. "Oh."

As the two women proposed ways that Beverly could go about finding a new partner, Trudy's mind again turned to Shawna. She imagined what it would be like if their friendship had resembled the one, she and Beverly had fallen so easily back into.

If Greg wasn't so controlling and constantly trying to push her out of Shawna's life, they could have hung out like this at each other's homes. Maybe then Shawna would have come to her when she needed an outlet, instead of feeling the need to go out and sleep with random men, and perhaps she wouldn't have tried to kill herself. Trudy had called the hospital while driving to Beverly's but was told Shawna had been released.

It also had not gone over her head that she had taken Shawna's place, and was now that friend that was pushing her other friend to start seeing men. Why were some women like that? Why did they feel that in order to be happy, there had to be a man in their life? But then again, Trudy wasn't pushing Beverly into a relationship, and it wouldn't hurt for her friend to get out and have a little fun.

"So, which dating app are we signing up for?' asked Trudy, laughing.

"A dating app? Whatever happened to meeting face-to-face? No," Beverly said, shaking her head. "I've never been one for online purchases. I prefer buying in the store. That way, I can actually see what I'm getting."

"Does that mean we're going out tonight?" Trudy prodded.

"Going out? I don't even know what that means." Beverly paused for a second, thinking. "Then again, maybe."

Trudy snuggled under the covers, relishing the feel of the weighted comforter and pillowtop mattress she was lying on.

If this is the type of bed that Beverly provides for her guest, what must the bed in the master bedroom be like?

She could get used to this.

Trudy glanced over at the clock on the nightstand. The time read twenty-one minutes after ten. She could not remember the last time she had slept so late.

Eventually, she had convinced Beverly to go out last night. Or had Beverly ended up convincing her? She was only joking when she mentioned it in the first place. But before she knew it, they had spent most of the afternoon going through Beverly's closet, looking for an outfit for her to wear.

After trying on a dozen or so, that Trudy would have

killed for, Beverly decided she had nothing to wear. They ended up going to the mall to buy new clothes for Beverly and getting mani-pedis for them both.

Trudy had tried protesting when Beverly insisted she join her, but Beverly had persisted, saying, "How does it look with me getting pampered while my friend sits back and watches?"

As unseemingly as it felt for Trudy to have Beverly pay for her, it had been nice to be spoiled, a little.

The dress Trudy had worn that night was nowhere as nice as Beverly's ensemble. But the evening was not about her, and besides, she was not looking for any extra attention. She already had two men to deal with. Beverly wore a light blue fitted pantsuit that left one shoulder and her midriff exposed. She made Trudy almost want to take up yoga.

From the moment they walked into the nightclub, it seemed as if every man there was vying for Beverly's attention. Trudy loved watching her friend's face light up from all the admiring looks she was receiving. She even observed looks from men who were there with other women, being cast in their direction.

A few men had tried engaging Trudy in conversation. However, none of them seemed interested in any of her answers to their questions. She figured they were only speaking to her because Beverly was otherwise occupied at the time.

Watching the scene play out reminded her of when they used to go clubbing back in college. Back then, they had both been in a relationship but had quietly kept that information to themselves. There had been no need to share anything that was going to hinder them from getting free drinks. It was a wonder that they passed any of their classes between clubbing and going out on dates.

She and Beverly had stayed at the club until almost midnight and spent another hour or two, back at the house laughing and gossiping, about all the different men they had encountered. Especially the one who had worn so much cologne, it had caused Beverly to gag every few seconds, never realizing it was he that was making her sick. But even with the limited selection, Beverly had come home with a few numbers and prospects to consider.

Trudy had been so tired that she skipped showering and brushing her teeth, and had simply stripped off her clothes in front of the bed before climbing in. She barely remembered falling asleep.

Right now, she could use a cup of coffee, but she should check in at home first. She picked up her phone from the nightstand, and saw that she had a text from Eric. "Hope you're having a good time," it said. There were also several texts and missed calls from Matt. Somebody was missing her.

She called the home phone, and Eric answered on the other end. "How's everything going?"

"Great, I was just watching TV. Dad's still asleep, and Cori left with Tara. You having fun?"

Trudy smiled, thinking that yes, she was actually having fun. "Yeah, baby, I'm having fun."

"Good," Eric remarked emphatically.

"I was just calling to check-in. I'll let you get back to whatever you were watching. Love you."

"Love you too, Mom."

Now to call Matt.

"Hey sexy," he drawled.

She felt her insides melt. She didn't think she could ever tire of being called sexy. "Hi, I see you called me."

"Hope it wasn't too much. I was missing you."

"No, not *too* much. Sorry it took me so long to call you back. I'm still in bed." Trudy slid back underneath the plush comforter.

"Wish I was there lying next to you."

"Mm," she moaned. "Me too."

"Okay, stop that. I just stepped out of a meeting to take your call. I have to be, um… be presentable when I go back."

"You started it," she chuckled.

"You're right. Not sure if you got my text or not. But, I was wondering, if you could set aside some time for me, during your little mini-vacation."

The whole purpose of this vacation had been to get some clarity on this anarchy that had become her life. And as much as she had enjoyed herself over the last day, the time away had merely been a distraction, and she was still as confused as ever. Even still, this was time she had set aside to visit with an old friend. How would it look if she suddenly took off?

"I'm not sure. I did just get here, yesterday. It might look suspicious if I were to disappear for several hours in a city, I'm unfamiliar with."

"What if I were to stop by for a visit, maybe meet your friend?"

Trudy suddenly felt anxious. Was he serious? "I don't think that would be a good idea. Beverly doesn't know about you," she whispered into the phone.

"Oh, I thought you girls told each other everything."

"No, we don't." Trudy admonished.

"Sounds like I hit a nerve. I was only kidding," Matt laughed. "At least only a little bit."

Trudy softened slightly. "Okay? If you say so."

"So, when can I see you? What about Sunday? We can spend some time together before you have to go back home."

She *could* leave a bit earlier than planned and meet Matt somewhere outside of the city. Somewhere, no one knew her, and she did not have to be on guard. "I suppose that would be okay."

"Great, I'll figure out a place and send you the address.

See you then." Matt said, ending the call.

A big grin stretched across her face as Trudy rolled around in the bed excitedly, already eager for Sunday. Okay, enough of that. As pleasing as it was to just lie there, she should get up and go seek out Beverly.

Beverly was sitting at her laptop taking a meeting when Trudy found her. She was still in need of coffee but did not want to disturb Beverly by rambling around her kitchen, searching for supplies. Also, she didn't know where anything was. She decided it might be best to look for coffee elsewhere. It would also give her the opportunity to see more of the area. Trudy went back to her room, showered, and got dressed before returning to the kitchen. She waved to let Beverly know she was leaving. Beverly smiled and waved back. Closing the front door quietly behind her, Trudy started out.

It did not take her long to find a coffee shop. A few were only minutes away from Beverly's house. She settled on a local store, wanting to lend her support to a small business.

Trudy drew in a deep breath as she entered the shop. She loved the smell of coffee brewing. How did anyone get along without it?

A few people were sitting inside, sipping coffee as they hacked away at their laptops—most likely writers working on their latest novel. The store was filled with incidental knickknacks scattered about. Coffee mugs, Birthday and get-well-soon cards, miniature carved wooden animals, handmade jewelry, kettle corn, and a few used books were strewn on top of one of the tables. Trudy assumed the assortment of items were from locals in the community trying to sell their wares.

She stepped to the counter, where she was greeted by a cashier, wearing a yellow smock and a helpful smile. "What can I get you today?"

Trudy scanned the menu, searching for something familiar. "A white mocha with three shots of espresso."

The cashier regarded her with a raised eyebrow, before reciting her order back and ringing her up. He handed Trudy her change and turned to prepare the order himself.

Trudy placed the change in a tip jar and then chose a book to flip through while sitting at a table to wait for her order.

Once the barista finished brewing her coffee, he walked over and handed it to her. Trudy took a sip. *Perfect.* She smiled and thanked him.

Outside, Trudy walked along the street, looking in at the shops that lined the road through the windows. She felt her back pocket vibrating and pulled out her phone. It was Mr. Dalsin.

Was he missing her already? She chuckled. "Hello."

"Hi, Trudy. Enjoying your vacation?"

"Yes. How are you doing today?" She would say it was unusual to get a call from her employer during her vacation, but how often did she take one?

"Well," Mr. Dalsin replied. "I'm not sure. I opened an

email from one of our suppliers, or at least I thought it was. It was an invoice for supplies, but the amount owed seemed a bit excessive."

"Who was the supplier?" Trudy asked.

"Saunder's Feed and Seed."

"Okay. What's today? The twelfth. Sarah doesn't usually bill us until the first of the month."

"Yeah, that's what she told me when I called. Evidently, whoever sent the email changed a few letters in the email address to make it look like it was from Sarah. Just glad I called her before I clicked on anything."

Trudy expelled the breath she had not realized she'd been holding. She would never have forgiven herself if her boss had lost money because she wasn't there. "I'm glad you caught it. Maybe have Dell, the IT guy, look into it."

"Great idea. I'll do that, as soon as I get off the phone with you."

"Now, I wish I hadn't taken a vacation."

"No, no. Don't you think like that. You deserve it. I have Peggy here, and she's double-checking behind me. She was the one who caught it. The main reason for my call was to see if anything like this has happened before."

Trudy searched her brain, reflecting over past emails and statements. "No, nothing. If there had been anything, I would have alerted you. You know what? I can come in today and check over the books and see if I missed anything."

"That is not necessary." Mr. Dalsin stressed. "Enjoy your vacation. It can wait. I'll do as you say and let Dell look it over."

"Okay." She wasn't sure how she was going to enjoy herself. More than likely she would spend the rest of her vacation, obsessing that she might have missed something like this in the past. But Mr. Dalsin was right; it would be best to leave it in Dell's hands for now. And that could take anywhere from a couple of hours or even days.

"I'll see you when you get back."

"But keep me up to date if you find anything."

"Will do."

Why would someone send an invoice in the middle of the month?

Trudy's brow was still knitted together when she got back to the house. She walked in and wandered right past Beverly when she opened the door without saying anything.

"Are you okay?"

"My boss called while I was out," Trudy said, speaking to no one in particular.

"They can't go a day without you, huh? Not even on the weekend." Beverly laughed lightly.

"Someone sent a fake invoice from an account that appeared to be from one of our vendors."

"Okay. Wow," said Beverly, surprised. "How much money is the company out of?"

Trudy turned to stare at Beverly as if she just remembered where she was. "Oh, no. Mr. Dalsin realized something was wrong before sending any money."

"Thank God for that." Beverly placed her hand over her chest. "So, everything's fine?"

"Yeah, I guess. It's just that… why send an invoice in the middle of the month that just… so happens, to be on a day that I'm not in the office?"

Beverly reached over and squeezed Trudy's shoulders. "I'm sure it was just a coincidence. Thankfully. it sounds like whoever sent the fake invoice is probably new to this. The important thing is it didn't work. You've got your IT person on it, right?"

"Yes."

"Great," Beverly said, not sounding convinced. Neither was Trudy. Come on, cheer up. This weekend is about getting away."

"You're right," Trudy said, trying to give Beverly a persuasive smile. "No harm nor foul. Everything's fine."

"Great. Now that that's out of the way, I have a big day planned for us. There is a little town not far from here, with a street filled with antique shops." Beverly

watched Trudy, waiting for her news to sink in.

This time, Trudy's smile was genuine. She couldn't believe Beverly remembered her love of yardsaling and shopping for antiques. Most of Trudy's furniture in their college dorm had been items she'd found on the weekends when she ventured out, while most other students were participating in sororities or involved in clubs.

Another roommate might have laughed at her, but Beverly was always curious to see any new discovery Trudy brought back or hear about some of the other impressive treasures she had come upon that day.

Beverly had never joined her on any of those outings when they were in college. Which made it even more endearing that she'd planned an activity such as this for their day.

It was nearly five o'clock before they left the last store. Beverly had not exaggerated about there being so many antique shops in the small town. They had spent most of the day walking in and out of shops and still had not covered the entire street. With there being so many stores left to peruse, Trudy made a mental note to come back in the near future for another visit.

Now, they were in the car, headed back to Beverly's house. Trudy had angled the passenger seat back and was gazing out the window. "Thanks for planning this," she said, casting a glance over at Beverly.

"It was my pleasure. I can't wait to find a place for that beautiful antique clock you stumbled across."

Trudy had found a bronze table clock with an ivory bottom, tucked away in the corner of one of the shops. On top of the clock's setting were the figures of a mother and child. The mother was kneeling with her arms outstretched towards her son, who was teetering towards her.

Beverly had come upon Trudy running her fingers along the folds of the tiny figures as she stared, mesmerized by the clock. It *was* beautiful. Beverly had encouraged her to buy it.

Knowing she couldn't afford it, she had feigned disinterest and placed it back on the shelf. After questioning Trudy several times to make sure she didn't want it, Beverly ended up purchasing the clock for herself. Despite the clock being worth more, the shop owner's asking price had still been pretty hefty.

"Yeah, it was kind of cute." Trudy shrugged her shoulders halfheartedly.

"We've had two activity-filled days. Maybe we should spend tomorrow just hanging around the house with our feet up."

"I was actually…," Trudy began, her voice faltering. "Going to head out a little earlier than I initially planned."

"Really?" Beverly took her eyes off the road for a second

to glance at Trudy. "I thought you had moved on from that work thing."

"Oh, no. It's just...I need to get back and check on the kids before school starts. Also, I need to get my dog from the kennel before it gets too late, and they end up charging me for another day."

"Okay. If you say so." Beverly reached over and squeezed Trudy's hand. "I know you are not leaving until tomorrow, but I'm really going to miss you."

"I'll miss you too," Trudy responded sincerely.

"But you'll be back. Right?" Beverly asked, giving Trudy a piercing glare.

Trudy laughed. "Yes, I'll be back. Now, please, put your eyes back on the road!"

CHAPTER 8

L EAVING BEVERLY'S HAD been bittersweet; part of her wished she could have stuck around and continued her escape from reality. Trudy was pretty sure that if she had wanted to stay longer, Beverly would have let her. Before leaving, Beverly had offered Trudy a job with a salary that was almost twice that of what she was making now. But the job was in the same town where Beverly lived, so of course, she would have to move. As tempted as it sounded, Trudy was pretty sure that, in no uncertain terms, would James consider moving that far away from his family and their business.

Not only did Trudy leave with a job offer, but Beverly also managed to sneak in a vintage clock before she left. While she was putting her suitcase in the trunk, Beverly went back into the house, mumbling that Trudy had forgotten something. She returned, cradling the clock in her hands. "Don't forget this," she'd said, grinning from ear to ear.

Trudy had tried to refuse the gift, saying it was too much and kept insisting she didn't even want it. But Beverly simply ignored her, walked over to the car, and gingerly placed the clock on the passenger seat. She then closed the car door with an air of finality that put an end to the conversation.

"Thank you," Trudy had finally said before giving Beverly a hug and saying goodbye. She watched her friend wave from her rearview mirror until she was no longer in her sights.

Although the trip was meant to be an escape, sadly, life had refused to be put on hold, and the incessant messages on her cell phone were a constant reminder.

Surprisingly, there were quite a few texts from Cori asking when she was coming home. Trudy had almost believed her daughter missed her, until she saw the messages were about needing money for a yearbook and senior pictures.

Despite assuring Matt that she was still meeting him, he had sent several messages to make sure she had not changed her mind. She supposed that absence made the heart grow fonder, although she suspected Matt's constant texts had nothing to do with his heart. It seemed it had had the opposite effect on James. She had not heard from him the entire trip.

Her destination's end brought her to a quaint Bed and Breakfast several miles outside of the city. Trudy would have thought she'd put in the wrong directions if she had not seen Matt's car parked outside. She had said she needed to be back home tonight, hadn't she?

Trudy was barely out of the car when she saw Matt running up to her. He pulled her into his arms and kissed her fully on the lips. Trudy was about to pull away before she remembered that no one knew her here. She leaned back in and willfully returned his kiss.

Mm, he tasted so good.

"I missed you," he said, coming up for air.

Trudy smiled cheekily. "I missed you too."

"You have any luggage you need to bring in?"

"About that. I did say I needed to be home later tonight, didn't I?"

"Yeah, yeah," Matt said, guiding her inside the house. "I just know that women like to have their things on hand."

Inside the Bed and Breakfast, Trudy was greeted by the owner, who was waiting for them in a small seating area with mixed-match furniture and a small fireplace. "Hello, Mrs. Kelly."

Trudy simply raised her eyebrow a fraction of an inch and nodded her head at the woman in acknowledgment. She was not sure what information Matt had given the owner, but she felt it was best to go along with it.

"Your room is ready, and as I told your husband—"

This time, Trudy giggled—well, more like snorted—but quickly covered her mouth in an attempt to suppress it.

"Told your husband," she continued. "That lunch would be served around noon in the dining area if you'd care to join us."

"Thank you." Trudy somehow managed to say without snickering. "The room?"

The owner pointed down the hallway, and Trudy took off with Matt in tow.

As soon as she got into the room, she fell on the bed, the laughter spilling from her. Matt lay beside her and held her until the outburst subsided.

"You done?" he asked.

"I think so," Trudy said, wiping tears from her eyes. "What's with the Mrs. Kellys?"

"I don't know." Matt shrugged. "I've never been married, figured I try it out to see how it sounded." He leaned down, drawing the tip of his tongue across her lips.

"Mm." Trudy moaned. She wrapped her arms around him, pulled him closer, and opened her mouth.

Matt pulled back sharply.

"What's wrong?" Trudy stared at him apprehensively.

"Oh, nothing. I just thought we would take things a little slower this time. We are out here in the middle of nowhere; no one is expecting you. We have time to enjoy ourselves."

Trudy pursed her lips together. "Looks like I'm going to need my *things* after all."

Matt smiled, giving her a look that said I told you so. "Thought so. Give me your keys. I'll get your bag."

She tossed Matt her keys and watched as he left the room in search of her supplies.

The room was a bit dated but clean. It appeared that the decorator was into florals. Everything from the comforter, to the throw pillows and rug were covered in wildflowers. Pictures of purple tulips and sunflowers hung from the walls.

Trudy got off the bed and made her way into the attached bathroom, to see if the room came with supplies, while she waited for Matt to come back. She was just stepping over the threshold when he returned with her suitcase.

"Thank you," said Trudy, grabbing her bag as she stepped back into the bathroom, closing the door behind her.

When she returned to the bedroom, she found Matt lying in the center of the bed with his legs stretched out and his feet hanging over the edge. He looked out of place in the full-size bed. Trudy wondered how the two of them were going to fit comfortably.

Matt moved from the bed when he saw her and motioned for her to lie down in his place.

Trudy climbed back into the bed, propped up the pillows, and stared up at Matt, a bit nervous. "You're scaring me."

"Nothing to be scared of," he said, smiling mischievously.

That smile had not reassured her. Now she was nervous and a tiny bit scared. The few times she and Matt had been together, albeit passionate, had still been hurried. Trudy was not sure that she could live up to the expectations that this little tryst entailed.

"That look on your face tells me something different." Trudy chuckled.

Matt sat down beside her, the mattress springs responding to the extra weight. "Trust me." He dipped his head and began planting little kisses in the crease of her neck, his hand running down the side of her torso.

Trudy sucked air through her teeth as her body jerked in response.

Matt sat up. "You okay?"

"Fine." Trudy smiled, her face clouded in desire. "That's just a tender spot for me."

"Noted," he said, taking back up where he left off.

Now that he had found her spot, Matt began an onslaught of attacks, nibbling and licking the tender area, creating a frenzy inside of her. Trudy fought the urge to cry out and pushed against him to stop. "No more. You're going to drive me crazy."

"Okay, okay," he said willfully. "Let's try someplace different." This time, he started his assault along her collarbone, loosening the buttons of her shirt, one by one, as he made his way down.

His trail of kisses stopped when he reached the lacy trim of her bra. He pulled the fabric down, exposing her nipple, and began stroking his tongue up and over the nub, causing it to pucker.

"Oh God," she whispered aloud. *What is he doing to me?*

She reached up to grab his head, but he pushed her hands away.

Was this some sort of ruse to drive her out of her mind? Because if so, Matt was doing a pretty good job. While he licked and sucked one nipple, he flicked his thumb over the other.

This time, Trudy tried to pull him on top of her. She was ready to move on past the foreplay; she wanted him inside of her. She needed him inside of her. Again, he protested.

He must want me, too. Right?

She reached her hand out, placing it between his legs. She pressed against his erection, and he groaned, biting down on her nipple. "Ssss," She arched towards him, sucking in air. "I want you."

"Say it again," he whispered in her ear.

"I want you," she said a little louder.

This time when he pulled away, it was to remove his clothing. Trudy quickly followed suit. Despite Matt's intentions to prolong their lovemaking, once they were naked, it was not long before it was over, and they lay twisted in the sheets, on top of the bed, trying to catch their breath.

"How many people do you think are in this house?" Trudy asked in between breaths.

"I'm not sure. Why?"

"I was just wondering how many people I have to avoid making eye contact with."

"Hm?"

"I'm sure we were loud enough to wake the dead," she laughed.

"Speak for yourself," Matt said, kissing her on the nose.

Trudy snuggled close to Matt, contemplating how long the two of them could hole up in the room before she had to worry about facing the other guest. She quickly remembered that it wouldn't be too long before she had to get back on the road to head home. She squeezed her eyelids together, hoping it would shut out the thoughts. She didn't want to think about that now. For now, she was Mrs. Kelly, and her only concern was Mr. Kelly.

Trudy rolled over on top of Matt, straddling him. "So, what does it take to get *you* to make some noise?" She smiled down at him impishly.

Their second time around had been as heated as the first, but Trudy had been unsuccessful at getting Matt to go any higher, than an octave above a whisper. However, she was pretty sure some sort of emergency service had been sent to check in on the couple down the hall, or at least a knock from the owner of the Bed and Breakfast was due pretty soon.

One of the side table lamps had been knocked on the floor. It seemed to be still intact, but neither of them had been brave enough to attempt to turn it on to test it out.

If the lamp was broken, Trudy was unsure how it could be replaced. Like the rest of the room, it was covered in a floral print, and there was no way a lamp like that was still in production.

Matt looked around the room, assessing the damage. "Good thing I purchased insurance."

"You did not?" Trudy stared at him wide-eyed.

"No, but from the looks of it, I should have. Who knew you had all this hiding inside of you?" he said, sweeping his hand around the room.

Trudy smiled self-consciously. "You bring it out of me."

"So, what you're saying is…that you like who you are

when you're around me?"

"I guess so. We have fun. Even if it is in secret," Trudy said, breaking eye contact.

Matt cupped her chin and turned her back to face him.

"What if it didn't have to be?"

"What's that supposed to mean?"

Matt shrugged. "I'm just saying. What if we could have fun together, in public, without you always looking over your shoulder all the time?"

"Well, right now, I'm *not* looking over my shoulder, and that's a good thing. But even that can't last forever. I thought *this* was only for a short time, and you would be headed back to Texas soon."

"I am, and…I want you to come with me."

"What?" Trudy stared at him, her mouth gaping open. "I have a family."

"I know, but I've thought about it. Your kids are, for the most part, grown up and can fend for themselves.

But," he said, when he saw her about to respond. "Your youngest, Eric, right? You can bring him with us."

"My son, who has never met you? Who doesn't know anything about this?" she asked, looking around the room. Trudy grabbed the blanket, pulling it closer to her. Although she was already naked, she suddenly felt exposed and needed something to cover herself.

"I know my plan isn't airtight, but I want you with me when I leave, and I want to make it as easy for you as possible."

Suddenly, the thought of running into strangers who were silently judging her was less intimidating than this conversation. Trudy needed to get out of the room. She jumped from the bed and ran into the bathroom, quickly getting dressed, and ignored Matt when he called out to her as she left.

The hallway and sitting area were clear, no prying eyes. There was a scent of something baking in the air. It must be close to lunchtime.

Behind the house was a grassy meadow that spread out for miles. Running through it was a little path that had been created from foot traffic over the years. Trudy made her way down the trail.

It wasn't long before she heard footsteps behind her. She didn't need to turn around to know it was Matt. He stayed back a few paces and remained silent, allowing her the space she needed. That simple little act was making it hard for her to ignore his earlier request. If she had walked away from James, he would have been more than happy to let her leave.

Trudy trekked on for several more minutes, comforted by his presence. Once she felt calmer, she stopped, turned around, and waited for him to come closer. "Why do you want me to come with you, anyway?"

Matt regarded her as if she were a bit slow. "Why wouldn't I?"

Trudy took a deep breath before responding. "No answering a question with a question. Remember?"

"I'm just saying…you are everything I could want in a person. You are caring, smart, and funny. And…you're not so bad in bed either," Matt added with a sly tilt of his head.

Although she was aware of the severity of the situation, Trudy managed a smile. "But you realize that with this half of the relationship…" she said, pointing at herself. "Things aren't that simple?"

"I suppose so."

Trudy looked at him, confused. "You suppose?"

"Why can't it be?" Matt reached out his hands to her. "Simple, I mean? You're not happy, except when you are at work or with me. Come with me and be happy. I'll even create a position for you at my company."

"That's easy for you to say. You are on the outside looking in. There are a lot of feelings to consider."

Matt regarded her, searching her face. "True, but what about *your* feelings? What do you want, Trudy?"

Matt turned around and walked back to the house, leaving her standing alone in the field.

As she stood there staring at Matt's retreating back, Trudy wondered.

What do I want?

Blue was excited to see her when she picked him up from the Vets. She missed him too and was eager for his affection. Trudy knelt down and hugged him as he pawed and licked her, with the assistant looking on.

"Ah, I hate going on vacation without my dog too."

"I think it's the first time I've ever left him. Did he do good?" Trudy asked.

"Yes, he was a good boy. Weren't you, Blue?" asked the assistant in baby talk.

Blue wagged his tail fervently, looking back and forth between Trudy and the assistant as if unsure whose attention he wanted more.

"Thanks for looking after him." Trudy tugged the leash a bit tighter, a little envious of the Vet assistant, and walked Blue out to the car.

She wondered how much she would be missed when she got home. Would they be as excited to see her as Blue had?

As much as she'd needed some time away, Trudy was ready to see her family and get back to work. Without her daily routine, she felt lost. She required consistency, and she needed her numbers.

Mr. Dalsin had called to say—well, she had ended up calling him. At home—that Dell had not found anything else unusual. That was good news. It had given her closure and helped to settle her nerves a bit. However, there was still Matt's proposal asking her to leave with him, and he would be gone in five days.

After he left her in the field, she continued to walk about half a mile and then turned back. She had found him in the dining area, having lunch with a few of the other guests. If any of them had heard them in the room earlier, they gave no indication and welcomed her to the table when she came in.

Trudy enjoyed listening to the other guests and hearing their stories of what had brought them to the Bed and Breakfast. Even better, she had a distraction that kept her from having to answer Matt's question.

The other couples were going out to pick apples later and invited Trudy and Matt to join them. As much as she had been tempted to go, Trudy declined the offer, knowing she had to leave soon.

Matt had been quick to step in and gave an excuse that they were moving about the country, visiting different Beds and Breakfasts, looking for a place to renew their wedding vows—someplace that could hold a few close family and friends. He even asked one of the men sitting at the table to take a picture of them to add to their photo album.

When they finally returned to their room, they both lay down on the bed, cuddling, neither of them saying anything to the other.

Eventually, the cuddling gave way to them making love. The other times they had been together had been simple acts of lust, a means of release. This time, it was slow and impassioned, like they were connecting on a deeper level, and in the midst of it, Trudy felt herself giving away a piece of her heart to Matt. This time, when she cried, it was not out of guilt but for the loss she felt.

When it was over, Matt wiped the tears from her eyes and laughed. "I guess I should have expected this."

Trudy regarded him without comment, not sure of what to say. Would it be appropriate to tell the man you were having an affair with that you were falling in love with him, and if so, what would be the point?

They had said their goodbyes not soon after. Matt kissed her on the forehead as she got in the car and told her he would be awaiting her answer. She nodded her assent before rolling up the window and driving away.

Before Trudy could pull into the driveway, Blue was already barking his head off. Maybe he was hoping they would hear him from all the way inside the house.

Either someone *had* heard him or had recognized the sound of her car because, by the time she turned off the ignition, Eric was standing at the front door. He ran to Trudy and gave her a big hug, almost knocking her down. "Woah," she said. "Have you grown since I left?"

"I don't think so," Eric responded, almost standing face-to-face with her.

He took hold of Blue's leash while she retrieved her bag, and the three of them walked into the house together.

James and Cori were sitting at the kitchen island, eating pork Lo Mein.

"Hey guys, I missed you," said Trudy.

James looked up, barely acknowledging her. Cori picked up her phone and started checking her notifications.

"The food smells good. Did you get any for me?" Trudy asked.

Cori laughed snarkily. "Um… we weren't sure when you were coming back."

Trudy frowned. "I called Eric when I left the Vets. I told him I was on my way here."

"Well, who knows if we can trust anything *you* say." Cori retorted.

Trudy felt as if she had been pierced with an icy dagger. Had they somehow found out?

"What are you talking about?" Trudy asked cautiously.

"The money for my senior pictures and yearbook?"

"What about it?"

"You never sent it." Cori glared at her.

Good, they didn't know.

"I don't know what you are talking about, Cori. I paid for your pictures and your yearbook. I have confirmations for both."

"Oh." For once, her daughter had the decency to look embarrassed. "I thought you were sending the money to me."

Trudy stood for a second, waiting. Surely, she would get more than an 'Oh,' especially, after the cold reception she had come home to. But Cori turned back to her phone without another word. "Is that all I get, an Oh? No, sorry, Mom. I apologize for jumping to conclusions, Mom."

"Okay!" Cori looked up long enough from her phone to roll her eyes. "Sorry."

"Wow, maybe I should have stayed where I was."

"Maybe you should have," said James.

Trudy looked at him, surprised. "That was harsh.

What is your issue with me? Was there a bill I forgot to pay?"

"No. We were just fine here while you were out running around doing God knows what."

"What is that supposed to mean? I told you where I was. You could have seen for yourself if you had bothered to call."

"I didn't want to interrupt your fun," James replied snidely.

"Yes, I was having fun. Is that a crime?" Trudy exclaimed.

Eric and Cori were staring at both their parents. It was not the couple's first argument, but it was the first one in front of them.

"It is in some states."

"To visit an old college friend?"

"If that's where you really were," James said, challenging her.

"I can call Beverly, and you can talk to her for yourself."

"Like friends don't cover for each other." James tossed his fork into the bowl of Lo Mein. "You know what, I've lost my appetite." He picked up his keys from the counter and left the house, slamming the door behind him.

"Just to let you know. If you and Dad get a divorce, I'm going with him." Cori smirked.

Trudy shook her head. "I'm sorry you had to see that, Eric."

He shrugged his shoulders. "Parents fight."

"Yeah, they do." Trudy picked up her bag. "I'm going upstairs."

Trudy had just finished sorting her clothes into two piles when she heard the front door open. James was back.

He walked into the bedroom slowly, his head hanging

down. Trudy remained silent, allowing him time to collect himself.

Finally, he looked up. "I'm sorry."

What could she say? He had every right to accuse her of stepping out on him, even if he didn't have any proof.

"It's okay," she said. "Already forgotten."

"No, it's not okay. You are this family's main provider, and I know that must be a lot of pressure on you. And now, when you finally take some time for yourself, time you deserve, you aren't in the house five minutes before I'm biting your head off. I'm surprised you even came back with the way we treat you around here."

Trudy pursed her lips together. "Like I said, it's okay. I've gotten used to it."

James came closer and dragged her to him. "That's not something you should get used to. You deserve more. A hell of a lot more than what I've been giving you lately."

Trudy could feel James's body shaking.

Was he crying?

James was saying all the things she had wanted him to say to her for years. Things she had just been begging for a few short weeks ago, but now they meant nothing. Even if the words he spoke were true, she could not find it within herself to care. It was as if the part of her heart that had once connected her to him no longer existed.

She supposed if he were crying, she should at least offer him comfort. It is what she would want someone to do for her. Trudy placed her arms around James and patted him tentatively on the back. "It's okay," she repeated.

James's hold on her suddenly went from that of someone in need of comfort to one filled with fervor. His hands began moving slowly down her back as he started planting kisses along along her neck.

Trudy felt her body stiffen. It was as if she were being groped by a stranger. "I need to get my clothes down to the laundry," she said, trying to pull away.

"Your laundry isn't going anywhere. I missed you." James pulled her hips against his erection to emphasize how much.

Oh, God. She felt so dirty. There was no way she could go through with this.

Knock. Knock. Someone was at the bedroom door. Trudy broke loose and nearly ran to the door to open it.

It was Eric. "Is everything okay?"

"Yes, baby. Everything is fine," Trudy responded, running her hands down the length of her clothes to smooth them. "Do you need anything?"

"No. Things were kind of quiet. I was just checking."

Eric shrugged his shoulders, then continued down the hallway to his room.

Trudy went to the bed and picked up her dirty laundry. "I need to get these things washed for the week." She looked at James apologetically before leaving the room.

As she placed her soiled clothing into the washing machine, Trudy reflected over what had just happened. James had wanted her, whether it was because he desired her or out of some need to assert his male dominance, because he'd felt threatened by her absence. But, regardless of his reasons, she had been repulsed by his touch.

For a mere second, she had considered pretending he was Matt just to get through it. But that would not have been fair to either of them.

Would this aversion to her husband pass in time, once Matt left, or would her body always crave his touch? Even now, with the memory still fresh of their time together this morning, she wanted to pick up the phone and call him. She *missed* him.

It felt great to be back at work. Mr. Dalsin seemed even happier to have Trudy back than she was, although he tried his best to hide it.

"Trudy, I can't say how much we missed you around here. Great to have you back." His eyes lit up, crinkling at the sides. His cheeks were so red, Trudy pictured him as a merry elf giving out Christmas presents.

It wasn't long before she became aware that he was, indeed, giving out presents. "I had not realized how much you actually do around here until you were gone. I would like to offer you a thirty-percent raise."

Trudy's mouth nearly fell open.

"I know it's been a long time coming," he continued. "But it is what you deserve, and the company can afford it. And of course, no one knows that better than you."

Mr. Dalsin stood patiently, waiting for Trudy's response.

She couldn't believe it. Just a few weeks ago, she was considering looking for a second job. Why she had not thought of asking for a raise was beyond her. And now that she was thinking about leaving the state altogether, he was offering her a bigger salary.

Well, she hadn't made up her mind about leaving, yet, and it would be foolish of her to turn him down if she were to stay.

"Thank you, Mr. Dalsin." Trudy walked from behind her desk with her arms extended. "May I?"

Mr. Dalsin nodded, then he and Trudy hugged. Somehow

the hug ended with Mr. Dalsin consoling Trudy when she broke down in tears.

"Everything okay?"

"Yes," she said, stepping away. "I'm just happy, is all."

"Well, I'm glad I had something to do with it. Would never have guessed you were even capable of crying. I didn't mean that in a bad way." He quickly explained when he saw the look on her face. "You just seem to be so formidable."

The atmosphere in the office had suddenly become uncomfortable.

"Well, I'll let you get back to your day." Mr. Dalsin began backing out of the room. "All the information from Dell's report is on your desk, and I'm sure you want to call your family and give them the good news."

Trudy watched as Mr. Dalsin left her office, glancing back at her awkwardly. For some reason, it did not feel like the kind of news she wanted to share with her family. Her first thought was to pick up the phone and call Shawna, so they could go out and celebrate. The only problem was, Trudy's number had been blocked from her phone. Surely Greg's handiwork.

But maybe it wasn't Greg, and Shawna no longer wanted to speak to her because she was mad about her showing up that day. Well, if she was, she was going to have to tell Trudy that to her face.

"Can I help you?" Greg stood in the doorway, looking at her as if she were an annoying tick he couldn't wait to get rid of.

"Yes, I'm Shawna's friend, Trudy."

"I know who you are,' he glared at her.

"I was wondering if I could speak to her."

"Shawna's not seeing any visitors right now."

Okay. Trudy knew the visit wouldn't be easy, but she didn't think it would be this hard. She was hoping that Greg wouldn't be home.

"I was just wanting to know how she was doing. I haven't spoken to her in a while."

"Oh, she's doing fine." Greg crossed his arms in front of him.

"That's great—"

"No thanks to you," he snarled, cutting her off.

"Me?" Trudy pointed at her chest, confused. "*I'm* the one that found her."

"Yeah. But…before *you*," Greg pointed back, circling his finger in the air. "She was happy with her life here. She had nothing to complain about. Then you showed back up, filling her head with ideas, making her think her life was miserable, and the next thing you know, she's trying to kill herself. That's on you."

Trudy stared at Greg in shock, trying to understand what she was hearing. She had done what? She had never tried to put any ideas into Shawna's head about her and Greg's relationship. In fact, it had always been the opposite.

"I'm not sure where you're getting your information, but that wasn't how things were between me and—"

"Whatever, I know how you women are." Greg stepped back, taking the doorknob in his hand. "You wasted your time coming here today. There's nothing for you here." He slammed the door in her face, ending their conversation.

What the hell just happened?

For the second time today, Trudy was in tears. Matt was right; it was becoming a habit. She needed someone to talk to, and the one person she shared everything with, was in a house ten feet away from her, and Trudy wasn't allowed to see her.

Trudy walked to the car, got inside, and closed the door behind her. She rested her head against the steering wheel, trying to compose herself. After a few minutes, she picked up the phone and called James. He would understand. Other than her, he was the only other person who knew all about Shawna and Greg's relationship. They had spent too many nights talking it over. He had always said he felt bad for Shawna but for Trudy to stay out of their marriage because it could end up backfiring on her. He had said to just be there for Shawna when she needed her.

Funny, she thought, laughing to herself as she listened to the phone ringing. She had kept her mouth shut, and still, it had backfired anyway.

Voicemail. Trudy looked at her watch. He must be asleep, with his ringer turned off.

She hung up and dialed again. This time, Matt picked up. She wondered how such a busy man always seemed to be able to make time for her. Well, he did own his own company.

"Hi," he said. "I'm not disturbing you, am I?"

"Oh, no. Just going over some paperwork."

"I'm sorry. I'll call you back later."

"Hey. I can tell you're upset. What is it?"

Trudy had left Shawna's and was now sitting at a stoplight. She wiped the tears from her eyes, causing the red light in front of her to blur. "I think I've lost my best friend."

"Your friend, Shawna, right?"

"Yes."

"Did something happen?" Matt asked cautiously. "She

didn't try to—"

"No, no. Nothing like that. At least, I don't think so. Her husband has officially banned me from seeing her. First at the hospital, now at home."

"That sucks. But maybe it's not him. Could it be a suggestion from her doctors while she is in therapy or something?"

"Hmph. I doubt it. It appears Greg believes I have been putting ideas in her head that have caused her to become unhappy, which then led to her suicide attempt."

"Wow."

"The thing is…hold on." Trudy grabbed a napkin from the armrest to blow her nose. "I would never do anything like that, and I know I'm being selfish, but I miss her."

"What about the woman you spent the weekend with?"

"Beverly? What about her?"

"Not saying she could replace your friend. But you still have her, right?"

"That's different. Beverly and I are just now reconnecting after years apart. Shawna and I have known each other since middle school. Besides, Beverly lives in a whole other town. It's not the same."

"Again, I'm sorry, and I wish there was something I could do to help."

"I know. I just needed someone to talk it out with." She was feeling a bit better now, and the tears had stopped. "But it might have helped if you had called her husband an ass for keeping my friend from me."

It's what James would have done.

"He's an ass. You want me to go over and rough him up for you?"

Trudy laughed. "No. But thinking of Greg with a black

eye helps.”

“Glad I could make you laugh. I do need to get back to this paperwork, though. That is if you’re feeling better?”

“Oh, yeah. You get back to whatever you were doing. Thanks for listening.”

“Anytime,” he said and hung up.

“Eric, when was the last time you saw your sister at school?” Trudy looked at her watch, checking the time.

She and Eric were playing a video game. It was mostly for show because Trudy had no idea what she was doing. Just pushing random buttons on the controller, hoping she found the correct one. So far, she had not. Eric had beaten her at every game except one, and Trudy was pretty sure he had felt sorry for her and let her win.

Trudy, James, and Eric had already eaten dinner, and James had gone to lie down afterward. The last family member, Cori, had not been heard from since she left the house this morning and was not answering her phone.

Eric was busy focusing on getting his car across the finish line and had yet to answer Trudy. “Eric, did you hear me?” she asked again.

“Sorry, Mom. She wasn’t at school today. It was Senior Skip Day.”

“And this is the first time I’m hearing about this?”

“It’s a thing.” Eric shrugged. “And besides, you don’t really want me snitching on my sister, do you?”

She opened her mouth to lecture him on something along the lines of being his brother’s—well, in this case, his sister’s—keeper but thought better of it. It wasn’t his fault that Cori wasn’t home.

Trudy picked up the phone to try her daughter again when she heard a car pulling into the driveway. She got up, walked to the front door, and opened it. Cori was getting out of Tara's car, and there were two boys in the backseat.

"Nice to have you home," said Trudy.

Cori walked into the house, ignoring her.

"You want to tell me why you didn't feel the need to let me know you were going to be late?"

Cori looked at her and rolled her eyes. "I messaged dad earlier."

And James had said nothing, even when she had remarked at dinner that Cori hadn't made it in yet.

"Well, nobody told me."

Cori shrugged her shoulders. "What's for dinner?"

"And what's this I heard about you skipping school today?" Trudy ignored the question. She probably would have let Cori slide on missing one day of school; she was a good student, and one day would not have hurt her record, but it was Cori's insolence that bothered her the most.

Cori stole a glance over at Eric, who quickly turned his head. "Why do you have to be such a…a…a…."

"Such a what?" asked Trudy, narrowing her eyes at Cori. "I've had a lot to deal with today. Greg won't let me see Shawna, and I've spent the rest of the day worrying about my daughter's whereabouts."

"It's not my fault you and Dad don't talk."

Their voices must have carried upstairs and awakened James. "What's going on down here? I'm trying to sleep?"

"The usual. Mom's unhappy with her life and taking it out on me."

"That is not at all what this is—"

"Enough yelling!" Please!" James shouted.

Trudy took a deep breath, ignoring his outburst. "From what I understand, Cori messaged you to say she was going to be late."

"Oh, yeah." James scrunched his face as if just remembering. "Sorry."

"You shouldn't have to apologize to her. She's only saying something because she wants to ruin my day just because hers was so bad. Just because she's not happy, she doesn't want anyone else to be either. No wonder Shawna doesn't want to speak to you anymore."

Trudy instantly felt the sting of Cori's words, and her hand flung out, landing against her daughter's cheek.

Cori stared at her mother dumbfounded, covering the red welt growing across her face, before running upstairs to her bedroom. The sound of a slamming door vibrated through the house. James ran upstairs after her. "Cori? Are you okay?" He called out.

Trudy stood in the living room, flexing the fingers on her right hand. She couldn't believe she had struck her daughter. She had never laid a hand on either of her children. She turned to find Eric staring at her.

"I'm sorry, Eric. I'm sorry." She grabbed her purse and removed her keys. "Tell your sister I'm sorry. I never meant to…" Trudy turned and left the house.

CHAPTER 9

THE DRIVE FROM the airport had gone smoothly. Trudy spent most of the ride staring in front of her at the back of the driver's head. Much of the city's view had been lost on her. She felt anxious, and her stomach was full of knots. Having one focal point had helped to keep her from going out of her mind.

She didn't want to show up at Matt's place with puffy eyes and streaks of dried tears on her face. This was supposed to be an exciting new beginning. Just last night, she had snuck out of the house with a small carry-on bag, leaving a note on the refrigerator door, addressed 'To My Family.'

After the confrontation with Cori, she had messaged Matt to find out when he was leaving. Unfortunately, he had already left. But once she'd told him she had decided to come with him, he purchased her a ticket, and she was on the next plane out.

Trudy knew the way she had left was cowardly, but it had been the right thing to do for her. She would never have been able to face them, and she wasn't needed there anymore anyway. Her only use to her family had been to pay bills and clean up after them.

What about Eric?

Eric would be okay. He had to be.

Only happy thoughts, Trudy.

She was here, and it was too late to run back home. She was sure they would have already read the note by now and if they had tried to call her, she didn't know; she had turned her phone off. Most likely, the only call would be from Mr. Dalsin after he received the email with her resignation attached.

"We'll be arriving in about ten minutes," the driver alerted her.

Trudy searched inside her purse for a mirror she remembered tossing in there years ago. Digging deep, her fingers eventually brushed against the compact.

Thank God.

She regarded the woman in the mirror. "It's okay," Trudy whispered to herself. "It's alright to do something that makes *you* happy from time to time. No one else is going to put you first but you."

Although the words sounded convincing, the woman staring back hadn't seemed to be persuaded.

"Did you say something, Ms. Allen?" The driver asked.

"Oh, no, sorry." Trudy laughed. She had not realized he could hear her.

A few minutes later, they pulled in front of a high-rise apartment building. A doorman walked over to the car and addressed the driver.

"Dropping off or picking up?" he asked.

"This is Ms. Allen," the driver said, rolling down Trudy's window as he looked back at her. "For Mr. Kelly."

"Ah, yes. Hello, Ms. Allen." the doorman said, acknowledging her. "Do you have any luggage?"

"Just my carry-on," Trudy said, pointing to the bag beside her on the floor.

The doorman opened her door, and she stepped out to allow him access to her bag.

Making sure the doorman and Trudy were clear of the curb, the driver tipped his hat. "Good day," he said and pulled away.

Trudy followed the doorman inside a spacious lobby, that only held a few chairs set against a wall, and a small table with magazines and newspapers on top.

He turned to her abruptly and introduced himself. "My name is Jerry. If you need anything, you can contact me or the night doorman, Corey, at the front desk at any time."

Corey. Trudy felt a stab at the place her heart should be, at the mention of her daughter's name. She pressed her fingers between her ribcage, hoping to ease the pain.

"If you will? Follow me." Trudy followed Jerry as he made his way to the elevators, rolling her bag behind him.

Once the doors opened, he and Trudy stepped inside. Jerry pushed the only button on the panel. It was labeled for the fifteenth floor.

His own private elevator?

Once they reached the top, the doors to the elevator opened, and Jerry waited for Trudy to step out first. She then followed as he made his way down the long, carpeted hallway. Trudy noticed that there were only four doors on the entire floor. One was for the stairs, another allowed access to the roof, and the others were for the only two apartments on the floor—one at each end of the hallway.

Jerry stopped at the door, marked 1501, and knocked. A few seconds later, Matt answered with a phone at his ear.

"Let me call you back," said Matt, ending the call.

"Trudy, you're here," he opened the door wider to allow her entrance into the apartment.

Trudy took her bag from Jerry and thanked him.

"Yes, thank you, Jerry." Matt reached into his pocket and placed something into the doorman's hand.

"Thank you, sir," said Jerry, with a slight bow.

"Welcome to my abode." Matt closed the door behind him.

The apartment was more extravagant than anything Trudy had ever seen. In the seating area, was a sofa and several plush armless settees, upholstered in white. The textured wood, end and cocktail tables, were adorned with expensive vases and Angelica crystal lamps. Everything looked expensive and breakable. Trudy could just picture herself marring the floors with her cheap heels.

"Nice," Trudy responded apprehensively. "I hope I don't break anything."

"Don't worry," Matt said, waving her off. "It can all be replaced. So, how was your trip?"

"It was okay."

"And the ride over?"

"Okay as well," Trudy answered, giving him a small smile.

"Well, I'm sure you could use some time to settle in."

Matt led Trudy to the first room at the beginning of the hall. It was sparsely furnished and appeared to be dedicated as a guest room.

"I'm not rooming with you?" Trudy asked, confused.

"Well, I thought that since we were still getting used to each other, you might feel more comfortable in your own space. For now," he added.

Trudy shrugged her shoulders and wheeled her bag into

the room. They had slept together several times, and she had left her job and family for him but, *they were still getting used to each other?* Maybe he was having second thoughts. If so, she didn't want to push it.

"I have to get back to the office. I only came home to make sure you didn't have to show up to an empty house."

Trudy stared at Matt, baffled. "You didn't take the day off? I thought we would be spending—?"

"No," he said, cutting her off. "I wasn't able to. There are some important matters I have to deal with. I'm on a deadline."

Trudy placed her suitcase on the bed, unzipped it, and began searching for something to wear. "Okay, just give me a minute to change. Might as well see where I'll be working."

"Um, no," Matt said, looking at his watch. "I really don't have time to wait." He walked over to her and kissed her on the forehead. "I'll see you when I get back."

Trudy looked on as Matt went back into the living room, grabbed a leather satchel, and left.

Now, what was she supposed to do in this large apartment all by herself? She could probably spend the day visiting the city, but it didn't appear that Matt had left a key. Trudy walked to the window of her bedroom and peered down at the street below. There were people walking by, many of them in business attire, most of them on their phones. A dog walker passed by with several dogs, pulling her about on their leashes. Soon, a few women pushing strollers followed, walking fast-paced together.

Trudy felt like Rapunzel gazing down from her high tower. She took a deep breath, moved away from the window, and began unpacking her clothes.

She wished there was someone she could talk to, but the

only person left was Beverly, and she couldn't call her. What would Trudy say when Beverly asked how things were going? "Oh, I just moved to Texas." And when Beverly asked how the kids were dealing with the move. How would that answer sound? "I didn't bring them with me. Actually, I took off in the middle of the night and left my husband *and* kids."

That wasn't the kind of news you opened up with, to a friend you just reconnected with. What would Beverly think of her?

The one person she needed to talk to wouldn't or couldn't answer her calls. Trudy needed Shawna. She missed her friend, and she knew Shawna would never judge her, no matter what she said or did or how much time had passed.

Tucked away in the corner of her bag was the clock that Beverly had given her. Trudy sat on the bed, cradling it in her hands as she listened to the sound of the seconds ticking away. The minute repetition had a calming effect. Again, she told herself that she had done the right thing. New was good; it would work out in the end. It had to.

She placed the clock on top of the chest of drawers, removed her toiletries from her bag, and stashed it in one of the bedroom closets. Now, to go check out the fridge. Trudy had not eaten anything since last night. Her stomach had been in knots from the time she made up her mind to leave the note.

There was enough food in the refrigerator to serve a small dinner party. Trudy chose the deli platter with sliced meats and cheeses near the back, and a jar of mustard to make a sandwich.

She sat down and placed the items on the kitchen counter, where she found an assortment of breads, from rye, white, and wheat to choose from. Trudy popped a pod into the coffee maker while she prepared her meal. She found some chips in the pantry and sat down to enjoy her lunch.

As she sat there, with only the sound of her crunching chips, she felt a bit unsettled. Trudy looked around for something in the apartment to play music, but nothing was visible, and she didn't feel it would be right to go through Matt's things. Instead, she turned her phone on to search for local radio stations and was accosted by an abundance of notifications.

There were voicemails, text messages, and email alerts. The text messages were from James and Eric asking where she was. James wanted to know how she could do this to her family, and a few offensive words were thrown in, about what kind of person she must be to have done something like this. Eric wanted her to come home, and there were no messages from Cori.

Mr. Dalsin had sent an email stating he was unwilling to accept her resignation and would be giving her a few days to change her mind. Trudy closed out the notifications and continued searching for a radio station; she would check her voicemails later.

After finishing her meal, Trudy cleaned up her dishes and placed the deli tray back inside the refrigerator.

What next?

She could try tidying up around the apartment, but it was spotless. Matt must have someone come in and clean during the week.

She could change out of her clothes.

It took Trudy two tries before she was able to find the bathroom. She had only intended to take a quick shower until she stepped inside. The bathroom was as big as her bedroom back home. The tub could fit two people comfortably. On the countertop was an assortment of scented bubble baths and bath bombs that Trudy could only assume were meant for her. She sniffed from the different bottles and chose the one that smelled like peaches.

Standing over the tub, she squeezed the shimmering pink liquid into the surge of water, and watched as it filled with bubbles. The whole bathroom was permeated with the scent of peaches. Once the tub was full, she stripped and slipped inside.

Heaven. I could get used to this.

As welcoming as the bubble bath was, it felt strange to be lounging in a tub in the middle of the day. Part of her anticipated a knock at the door from someone who needed her to do something. Also, it was not in her nature to sit still for too long. If she was not sitting in front of a computer working, she needed to be moving, keeping busy.

Trudy closed her eyes and tried meditating, being in the moment, but her mind refused to quiet itself. She let out a long sigh, washed up, and drained the water from the tub. She would get dressed and call Matt to see if there was an extra key somewhere she could use. She had to get out of here.

When she opened the screen on her phone, she saw that there were more messages from James. This time, he was threatening her with divorce with willful abandonment. He was giving her until the end of the week to reach out to him, or he would be retaining a lawyer.

She quickly exited the message. She did not want to deal with this right now. Trudy dialed Matt. After two rings, it went straight to voicemail. He was ignoring her call.

Just a few days ago, he would have walked out of a meeting to talk to her.

She was probably overthinking it. It was one ignored

phone call. He must be in the middle of something important; otherwise, he would have answered. Trudy wished she could find out what this big project was, or at least get settled into her new job.

She thought about just showing up at the building but decided against it. It might be awkward, especially, if Matt had not gotten around to adding her name to the list of employees. With an organization of its size, she would not make it past the receptionist. And even then, how would she introduce herself at the front desk? "Hi, I'm Trudy, the current woman living in Mr. Kelly's apartment. Would you let him know I'm here?"

Or she could find something else to do with her day. Either way, Trudy would need a key. She supposed she could try calling the doorman and see if there was an extra one she could use. He should remember her.

Trudy searched through her phone and found a number for the building. Her call was answered on the first ring. "Alivia Towers, this is Jerry. How may I help you?"

"Yes, hi. This is Ms. Allen. The woman you helped earlier, in the apartment on the fifteen floor?"

"Yes, ma'am. I remember you."

"I was wondering…I want to go sightseeing, but I don't have a key to the apartment. Is there an extra key or a way for someone to let me back in when I return?"

"No, there is not an extra key that I can give you, but yes ma'am, I or the night doorman, depending on when you return, would be able to assist you with reentry."

"Great. Thank you so much."

"You are more than welcome. Is there anything else I can help you with?" Jerry asked.

"No, that was all," Trudy was just about to end the call

when she thought of something else. "Wait. Any suggestions on places to see that are nearby? Within walking distance?"

"Well, there is the Modern Art Museum. But we could have a car available if you would like to venture out further or do some shopping."

Shopping would be nice, but she didn't have money to buy anything. She had not felt comfortable walking out on her family and taking money from their joint account as well.

"No shopping for today. I'll be staying close by until I get more familiar with the city."

"As you wish, ma'am." Jerry hung up the phone.

The sidewalk was still crowded by the time Trudy made it downstairs. Everyone seemed to be moving twice as fast as she, but most of them steered around her as if she were a shrub that was planted as part of the landscaping.

Unlike the people who passed by, she was in no hurry. She had no idea when Matt would get back from the office, and other than responding to the messages piling up on her phone, her schedule was empty. However, before leaving, Trudy had responded to Eric and told him she loved him and would call him when she got settled.

The museum was only a few blocks from Matt's apartment building. On the ride there, Trudy had been too nervous to even glance out the car window. But now, she took in the city and was amazed at the architecture that surrounded her.

She had never considered living in the center of town like so many people seemed eager to do these days. But as she took in the building's designs, Trudy could see herself changing her mind. Each building stood out, unique from the one beside it. Where one was composed using natural stone, another was constructed utilizing smooth neutral panels with a pop of color in the center. They were beautiful. She felt as if she were walking down an aisle in an antique shop, where the wares were bigger than she.

Trudy found it curious as she watched the people passing by, that they never looked up. What was the point of living in the midst of all this if you never saw it?

The museum was in complete contrast to the city streets. It was a modern-day museum, a bit esoteric for Trudy's taste. She had been more moved by the building itself than most of the artwork inside.

One of the museum's alcoves housed an art display of a tottery wooden ladder, that appeared to be suspended by a fastening at the top of the ceiling. The ladder undulated as it rose from the floor. It reminded Trudy of the story "The Ladder of Rickety Rungs" by T. C. O'Donnell.

Much of the museum's works were installation art. The medium where pieces brought in and set up to showcase the artist's vision. Trudy preferred art that was created by the artist's hands, molded into something tangible.

But there was one exhibit that caught her attention. It was a display featuring collages. The collages were designed using the small papers that were placed on the hair by beauticians before processing chemicals. The artist's incorporation of the papers, along with his use of tertiary colors, gave the canvas the illusion of small brush strokes when Trudy stood back several feet away to view it. The one entitled "Eve" was her favorite.

She was just about to enter another exhibit when she felt her phone vibrate. Trudy was hesitant to check it but realized the call might be from Matt. It was. He had left a message saying he would be back from the office around 2, and maybe they could order a late lunch and spend some time together.

Trudy checked the time on her phone and saw that it was 11:45. That would give her about two hours. That would allow her a few more minutes to view another exhibit, and then she could see a little more of the city before heading back to the apartment.

Trudy had not had any problems finding her way back. Unfortunately, Jerry was on his lunch break when she returned but had left instructions with the doorman taking his place to let her back in.

It was now 3:30, and Trudy was sitting on one of the sofas, staring at the door, waiting for it to open. Matt was an hour and a half late and had not called or messaged to let her know anything. She had gotten up a few times and looked down at the street to see if she could catch a glimpse of him, but her explorations had been unsuccessful.

Trudy was playing a game on her phone when the door finally opened. She tried to compose her face to keep the frustration she was feeling from showing.

"I'm home." Matt rang out.

Even though she was mad, part of her wanted to run over and greet him, but she still wasn't sure about the protocols involving their relationship, so she sat there wringing her hands nervously.

"Sorry, I'm late. I know I should have called. But...I still thought you would be happy to see me." Matt walked to Trudy with his arms outstretched.

Trudy went to him, and allowed him to hold her. "Mm," she leaned in further. She had missed this.

Matt pulled back abruptly. "Let me get out of these clothes." He went to his bedroom and closed the door behind him.

It was twenty minutes before Matt returned to the living room. Trudy kept herself busy listening to music and walking around the apartment to get in the last thousand steps she needed to reach her daily goal.

Matt was dressed in a white linen shirt, a pair of loose-fitting khaki shorts, and barefooted.

Although he'd said they were going to order their lunch in, Trudy had not taken him literally. "So, what's for lunch?" Trudy looked down at her watch. "Make that dinner."

"I was thinking Thai," Matt said, opening one of the kitchen drawers and pulling out a few menus. "If that is okay with you?"

At that moment, Trudy felt she could eat cardboard if there was enough sauce to cover the taste. She had not eaten since this morning. Worried, even as she sat here waiting on Matt, that if she had eaten anything it would have ended up spoiling her appetite. "Sounds great."

Matt began placing the order with the restaurant while Trudy looked over the menu. However, he hung up without asking her what she wanted.

She placed the menu back in the pile with the others and went in search of plates and glasses in preparation for the food's arrival.

When the food came, Matt and Trudy sat at the kitchen island on opposite sides facing each other. Matt removed three containers from the takeout bag, placing each one in front of him. Once the bag was empty, he tossed it and began serving himself. Trudy sat silently and watched.

"What's wrong?" Matt asked when he noticed she

remained immobile.

"I wasn't sure if any of this was for me," Trudy said, waving her hands around. "Seeing you never asked what I wanted." she snapped.

Matt took a few seconds before answering as if collecting himself. "You're right. I apologize. Again, I wasn't thinking. I'm used to ordering for myself. If you want something else, I can order it.' Matt stood up. "The menus are—"

"No, that's okay," said Trudy. "I'll be fine with the dumplings and the Sesame chicken. I mean, if you're done with it," she added, seeing that he had placed most of it on his plate.

"You're welcome to the rest of it," Matt said, handing her one of the containers. "So, what did you get into while I was out today?"

Trudy had just placed a dumpling in her mouth and waited until she was done chewing to answer. "I walked to the museum."

"Did you enjoy it?"

"It was okay. I'm not really into New Age art. I'm more traditional. But one of the pieces stood out. It was called Eve."

"I'm glad you were able to find something to fill your time. I apologize," he said, giving her a hint of a smile. "For having to leave the way I did this morning."

"It's fine," said Trudy, shrugging. "It's in the past."

"So…" Matt started slowly. "How's everything on the home front? Have there been a lot of phone calls or messages?"

"James and Eric have left a few. None from Cori. James is threatening to file for divorce and abandonment if he doesn't hear from me soon. And Eric…" she trailed off, unable to finish.

Matt nodded as if he understood her hesitation. "So, anything from Mr. Dalsin?"

"Just a message saying he refused to accept my resignation and that my job would still be there if I wanted it."

"That was kind of him. Anything else?"

Trudy frowned. "What? With my family or Mr. Dalsin?"

"Either," Matt responded with indifference. "I'm just trying to figure out how you're doing."

"No, nothing else. But then again, I haven't really checked my phone much today."

"That's understandable. So," asked Matt, changing the subject. "Were you able to get in any shopping today?"

Trudy shook her head slowly. "Shopping? No."

"Sorry. I assumed with the new job, you would have considered maybe upgrading your wardrobe?"

Trudy looked down at the clothes she had selected when thinking they would be going out to eat—a long green sheer pullover and a pair of what she perceived to be fashionable, dark-wash jeans. Of course, both the blouse and jeans were most likely ten years or older. She then looked at what Matt had chosen to wear for just lounging around the apartment. The simple ensemble easily cost more than three times that of hers. Maybe more than all the clothes she had brought with her.

Was her wardrobe the reason he had not wanted to take her with him to the office today? Or why he had wanted to have their meal delivered? Was he ashamed of her? Her wardrobe had not seemed to matter before. But then again, they had been on her turf. Now, she was on his.

"I suppose that makes sense, but I don't have money for

new clothes," Trudy answered.

Matt regarded her quizzically. "Were you not employed up until yesterday?"

Trudy nodded her head.

"I know that your salary wasn't anywhere near what most accountants would earn, but it should have afforded you enough for a few sensible outfits."

Trudy cast her eyes down. "I suppose so, but having to support a family doesn't make it easy to afford nice things and…I didn't think it appropriate to take any money with me when I left. I wanted to make sure they would be okay."

"But doesn't your hus… um, James, earn a decent income working in Heating & Air?"

"Not really. He works for his family. And sometimes, there are weeks when he doesn't get paid if they do not pull in enough revenue that month. We mostly relied on my income."

"Oh," Matt replied as if suddenly everything made sense. "No wonder it was so…" he trailed off. "You know what. I could take off a few hours tomorrow morning and take you shopping for a few things."

"Oh, no." Trudy looked up, meeting his eyes. "I couldn't possibly."

"Let me. You came here for me. It's the least I can do. And besides, it's an investment. If you don't have a new wardrobe, you can't work. If you can't work, you can't buy new clothes."

Well, she could work. Trudy thought. But she got it.

"Thank you." Trudy smiled. "I'll pay you back when I get my first paycheck."

"You really aren't used to people doing things for you, are you?" Matt shook his head. "You don't need to pay me back.

It's a gift."

After finishing their meal, the two of them washed up the few dirty dishes and put them away. "It's still early. How about we watch a movie before bed?" Matt suggested. "Although, I may need to lie down a little earlier than you. I have some work I need to go over before we head out to go shopping in the morning."

Trudy followed him into the living room and settled on the couch. She watched as Matt opened a hidden drawer in the coffee table where he had the remotes stashed. "That's where you keep them hidden," she laughed.

Matt sat down beside her, and Trudy curled up on the couch, leaned towards Matt, and laid her head on his shoulder.

He smiled down at her but said nothing. He pushed a button on the remote, turned on the TV, and began switching through the guide before settling on an action movie. Again, Matt had chosen something without asking her opinion. Trudy lifted her head, ready to protest, but dismissed it. It was a movie she had wanted to see anyway.

She settled her head back down on his shoulder and breathed in the herbal, earthy scent of the soap he'd used when he showered.

Nice.

She moved in closer and placed her hand on his thigh.

Matt laid his hand on top of hers and slid it down to the cushion beneath them. "You know we've gotten to know each other on a level that's mostly sexual. Maybe for the first couple of weeks, we could take things slow?" he asked, raising one eyebrow.

Trudy sat up, stretched her legs out, placed her feet on the floor, and slid over a few inches.

Shouldn't I be the one saying that?

He had pursued her for weeks until she'd given in, and now that he had her, he wanted to take things slow? Was she living in some sort of alternate universe?

If that was how he felt, then she would have to respect it. She would want the same from him if it were the other way around. Besides, there was nothing wrong with what he was asking. Perhaps he wanted to see if the way she felt about him was real.

"Sure, we can do that." Trudy drew her lips back into a smile.

Trudy awoke on the couch with a blanket thrown over her. She must have fallen asleep during the movie. She peered around the room, trying to make out the shapes.

What am I doing here?

If Matt had not shown back up after all these years or if he had just cast her a simple wave in passing, what would she be doing now? Trudy had left the life she'd spent almost twenty years creating—her and James's anniversary was just a few weeks away—for what she thought would be a life of excitement, with a man who just a few days ago couldn't seem to keep his hands off her. And now she was lying on a couch, by herself, with him in a bedroom just a few feet away at the end of the hallway.

"You just need to find something to worry about," Trudy whispered aloud. "It's just your nature."

That's all it was—looking for problems when there were none. Anyway, it had been decades since she'd been with someone new. Maybe dating had changed.

Trudy knew what her problem was; she required

something to ground her. She needed to be working. She couldn't remember the last time she didn't have anything to do. She felt so aimless. But things would be better tomorrow. She would find some new clothes, and then she could start her new job.

The next morning, Trudy found herself again waiting on Matt. He spent most of the day holed up in his room, on his computer and making phone calls. She made a cup of coffee for breakfast and tried reading a book on her phone while she waited.

He stuck his head out a few times to tell her it shouldn't be too much longer. In the end, they didn't leave the apartment until after eleven o'clock.

Trudy wondered what it was about this new account that was keeping him so busy. Although she was going to be working with him soon, he never talked about his work. Whenever she asked him about it, he would only say it was some big business account he had been after for a while. Why all the secrecy? Of course, she knew that depending on the size of the account and whether there were other companies interested, he had to worry about certain information leaking out. But who was she going to tell?

All this secrecy was making her question what she knew about Matt. Other than what was written about him on his company's profile and what she knew about him from years ago, she realized she didn't know much. Maybe his decision to take things slow was not a bad idea after all.

There was a car waiting for them outside the building. Behind the wheel was the same driver that had picked Trudy up from the airport.

"Hi," said Trudy when she recognized him.

"Good morning, Ms. Allen." He tipped his hat before getting in the driver's seat, and closing the door behind him.

Matt ended his call and slid over on the seat beside her. "Okay, I am putting my phone on silent. The rest of the morning is yours." He leaned over and kissed Trudy on the cheek. "Where to?"

"I have no idea," answered Trudy. "Remember, I'm new here."

"That's right. Robert," Matt said, speaking to the driver. "The lady needs new clothes. Any suggestions?"

"Yes," Robert said, glancing back at Trudy. "I know the perfect place."

Robert took them to a few shops outside of town, where Trudy was able to find several outfits that Matt, after watching her try on all of them, deemed suitable for the office. While she was in the dressing room, he picked out a few casual items for her as well.

One of his selections was a teal green dress with half sleeves that buttoned up in the front, with a skirt that belled out above her knees. Matt removed the price tag before handing it to the saleswoman and suggested Trudy wear the dress out for lunch.

The dress was not in the style of anything she was used to wearing, but after trying it on, Trudy saw that it suited her. She also noticed that the dress was a size smaller than normal, and that she had lost a few pounds.

For lunch, Robert drove them to a small Italian restaurant about twenty minutes further out. They had just missed the lunch rush, so there were only a few people inside. Because the restaurant was so empty, the hostess allowed them to choose their seats.

Trudy noted the huge windows at the front that faced out towards a flower garden of yellow roses and oriental lilies, but Matt pointed out a table at the back of the restaurant, near the restrooms.

Once they were seated, the hostess handed them the menus and left with instructions that their waiter would be with them soon.

Trudy picked up her menu and scanned it. "So, what's good here?"

"Um…" Matt said, glancing down at his menu. "I'm not sure. I asked Robert to pick the restaurant. I've never been here before."

"Is that something you usually do?" asked Trudy. "Pick out new restaurants to try?"

"I guess you could say that," Matt murmured.

"With a city this big, I can imagine—"

"Matt." A tall man wearing a rather expensive tailored suit walked over to their table. "Funny seeing you here."

Trudy watched as the color drained from Matt's face.

While the man waited for Matt to respond, he nodded at Trudy and smiled.

"Ah, Brian," said Matt, finally finding his voice. "Well, you know. Sometimes, you have to venture out and try new things. What brings you…why are you…I mean, do you come here often?" Matt laughed uncomfortably.

Trudy had never seen Matt so flustered. He always seemed so sure of himself.

"Well, I took the day off. You too, it seems." Brian said, looking at Trudy. "It's my wife and I's anniversary. This is the first restaurant I could afford to take her to. It's kind of a tradition."

When Trudy saw that Matt was not going to respond, she turned to Brian. "Happy Anniversary."

"Thank you." Brian smiled down at her.

"Yes. Happy Anniversary." Matt chimed in. "This is Trudy. Trudy, Brian. We were just having a business lunch. Trudy is interested in coming to work for us."

Business lunch?

Matt's odd behavior, the restaurant, and the choice of seating were starting to make sense. He had not wanted them to be seen together.

"Oh, I apologize. I hadn't realized. I'll let the two of you get back to your lunch. See you back at the office tomorrow. Nice to meet you, Trudy." Brian left, but not before giving Trudy the thumbs up and mouthing the words 'Good Luck.'

The waiter had been waiting for Brian to leave before taking their order. And Trudy thought it best to wait before addressing Matt about this strange interaction. She now had a headache and was no longer hungry, but she ordered a Caesar salad and a glass of white wine anyway.

Evidently, their encounter had not had the same effect on Matt as it had had on her. He ordered a steak and potato, along with a bottle of the House red wine.

"I guess you weren't very hungry," Matt replied when the waiter left.

"Kind of lost my appetite."

Matt looked at her, raising an eyebrow. "Oh, yeah?"

"Yeah. So, what was that about?"

"What was *what* about?"

"I see we're back to answering a question with a question." Trudy crossed her arms in front of her. "The thing with Brian. This little hideaway restaurant and the business lunch." Trudy said, using air quotes. "Are you ashamed of being seen with me? Why did you bring me here?"

"Robert thought it was a nice restaurant."

Trudy shot him a heated look. "To Texas. Why did you bring me to Texas?"

"It's not like that, okay?" Matt sighed. "First, I don't want people at my company knowing my personal business. That was why I said it was a business lunch. That's the reason for the hideaway restaurant. Second, I brought you to Texas because I want you here," he said, meeting her eyes.

"Then, why the distance?" Trudy asked, trying to keep the hurt from her voice. "Why the separate bedrooms?"

"I've explained that already. We are getting to know each other."

His explanations made sense, but for some reason, Trudy felt she was not getting the whole story. Something was off.

"Looks like I am going to have to go to the office and get ahead of the gossip. Brian likes to talk."

"Am I coming with you?" asked Trudy.

"Well, no. Not today. How would it look if you showed up in the middle of the day, especially right after our business lunch, that I'm sure Brian couldn't wait to fill the entire office in on as soon as he walked away. No. It may be a few more days before you begin work. And I suppose I'm going to need your resumé."

A crease formed in Trudy's forehead. "Why haven't you asked for it before now?"

"I was going to bring you in as sort of a...." Matt trailed off. "I don't know. I don't know why I haven't asked before now." He shook his head, a bemused look on his face.

Again, Trudy wasn't getting the whole truth.

"Let's just enjoy our meal. Okay? Everything is fine. Everything is still okay." Matt said the words more to himself than to Trudy.

Trudy spent the rest of lunch picking over her salad.

CHAPTER 10

I T WAS A LONG ride back to the apartment. Most of it was spent with Matt making phone calls while still trying to reassure Trudy that things were going to work out. She wasn't sure what any of that meant.

He could have saved it anyway. Trudy wasn't paying him any attention. Her head was in a fog from all the wine she'd drunk. She had consumed the one glass of wine she'd ordered, and almost half the bottle Matt had ordered for himself.

There was a little too much going on that she wasn't sure she wanted to face right now. The fog was safer for the time being.

They pulled up to the curve in front of the apartment building. Robert got out and walked to the side of the car and opened the door for Trudy.

Although Matt's side was facing the street, he let himself out.

Trudy sat in the car, staring at the sidewalk. *Why was it so far away?* She placed her foot outside the car, but for some reason, it hadn't touched the ground. It was as if she had forgotten how to stand.

How much have I had to drink?

"May I?" Robert asked, extending his hand out to her.

Trudy looked up and nodded her head slowly.

Robert reached into the car and grasped her elbow. "Just lean on me," he whispered in her ear.

"Is everything okay?" Matt asked from the sidewalk, still on the phone.

"Yes, sir. Everything is okay, sir." Robert called back.

Trudy placed her hand on Robert's shoulder as he lifted her effortlessly to the sidewalk and held her until she was steady on her feet.

"You got it now?" Robert asked, searching her eyes.

"I think so," Trudy answered. "Thank you." She wondered how often he had to help inebriated women out of his car.

Robert reached back into the car to retrieve her bags and set them down beside her. "Good day," he said, tipping his hat before walking away.

"Jerry, do you mind grabbing her bags and bringing them upstairs?" Matt asked the doorman, who had been standing by waiting patiently.

"Yes, sir," said Jerry.

When Trudy appeared unable to move any further, Matt walked over, took her elbow, guided her through the lobby and to the elevators.

Inside the apartment, Trudy took the bags and stumbled to her room to put her clothes away. She heard Matt mumble—at least it seemed like he was mumbling—something about going to the office and seeing her later.

Trudy noticed her clock on top of the chest of drawers had been moved, as well as some of the toiletries she'd left out earlier. The cleaning person must have come in while they were out today. Trudy wondered if the whole ruse of getting her out of the apartment had been to keep another person from seeing her.

She would have to think about that later; the alcohol was starting to take further effect on her senses, and she was getting sleepy. Trudy left the bags on the floor, telling herself she would put the clothes away later, and crawled into bed.

Trudy opened her eyes. The time on her Fitbit read 11:03. She reached over, feeling the other side of the bed. It was empty.

James must have left for work already.

She tried turning her head, but it was throbbing. It was a few more seconds before she realized where she was. She was not lying in the bed that she shared with her husband of nineteen years. She was in the guest bedroom of the man she had left him for.

Trudy pulled herself up slowly and rested her back against the headboard. She'd had too much to drink at lunch and had slept away the rest of the day.

Not like I had any place to be anyway.

Trudy laughed a little to herself, causing the dull ache in her head to flare up. "Ow." She reached up and placed her hand against her forehead.

She was going to need something for a hangover and 'yuck,' a toothbrush. The taste in her mouth was dreadful.

Trudy stood up on the side of the bed and held on to the nightstand until she was steady. She took a few steps and then tripped over the bags that she'd left on the floor. Luckily, she was able to catch herself before she fell.

She thought about turning on some lights, but they would

probably only make her headache worse. And speaking of her headache, she didn't think she'd brought any pain medicine with her. There might be some in her purse, but she didn't feel like searching through it.

Maybe Matt had some in his bathroom. A day ago, she had felt self-conscious about rifling through his things. Right now, she could care less. If Matt had something he wanted to hide, he better hope he had done a good enough job of hiding it.

A light was on somewhere in the kitchen, which made the trip down the hallway a lot easier than the one inside the bedroom.

Inside the bathroom, a medicine cabinet was situated on a wall near the sink. Within it were a few bars of soap, mini bottles of shampoo, conditioner, and mouthwash—things one would find in a hotel bathroom. At the very top was a small bottle of pain medicine.

Either Matt wasn't human and did not require things like razors or deodorant, or this was not his bathroom.

His must be in his bedroom.

She was curious to see what it looked like.

Trudy quickly swallowed down the pills but took her time brushing her teeth. It took flossing and swishing several mouthfuls of mouthwash before she was able to rid herself of the sour taste. She did not think she would be drinking again anytime soon, at least not in the excess she had this afternoon.

She placed the toothbrush back in its holder and took a deep breath. Now, it was time to check out Matt's room. She tiptoed down the hallway, trying to be quiet. It was probably unnecessary. The hallway's carpet was reinforced with extra padding, and Matt most likely wasn't even there.

Trudy tried the bedroom's door handle. It gave way

easily in her hand. The room was dark like hers and had thick pleated curtains covering the windows to block out the sun. She searched the shadowed corners' inner recesses and determined the room was more than twice the size of the guestroom.

Trudy was able to make out a seating area to the left, near the back of the bedroom. In front of her, about ten feet away, was a king-size bed, and to her right was another door that she believed to be the bathroom.

Stealthily making her way to the door, she saw that it was cracked. Worried that it might squeak, Trudy pushed it open a fraction more, allowing only enough room for her to squeeze through.

It *was* a bathroom. It was about the same size as the one she'd been using, but it did not include a bathtub—only a walk-in, ceramic tiled shower with a bench inside that spanned the entire wall.

At the back of the bathroom was another door that led into a huge Master Suite closet with a center island, wall shelves, and custom cabinets. Every inch of it was filled with Matt's clothing and shoes. Trudy had never seen so many clothes in one place outside of a department store.

And every inch of the room, held his scent. She walked over to the section where he hung his dress shirts and ran her hand across the fabric. She pulled one of them to her, breathing in his essence.

Another effect from the wine, weighing on her now that her headache was almost gone, was desire—the desire to be touched, to be held, the desire to be made love to. She ached for it, and it did not help that she was in Matt's closet so near to all his things.

Trudy made her way out of the closet and bathroom. She

was walking past the bed when she heard movement. She turned back and ran her hands over the covers and felt a familiar shape underneath.

Matt was home. He was here, and she was here.

It won't hurt to climb into the bed beside him.

If he awoke and asked why she was there, she would say she was scared and lonely. Part of that was true. He would have to kick her out if he didn't want her here.

Trudy walked to the other side of the bed, slipped off her dress, and climbed in. She laid still for a few minutes, making sure he was still asleep. When he began to snore lightly, she slid over and placed her head on his chest.

Matt turned over in his sleep and tossed an arm over her. Trudy snuggled in closer, wrapping an arm around his waist. Her hand touched against bare skin. Trudy hadn't realized that Matt slept in the nude.

She ran her hand across his lower abdomen, brushing against the hairs that tapered at his naval.

"Mm," Matt moaned in his sleep. Trudy, feeling confident, moved her hand lower.

She placed the palm of her hand on top of his erection and felt it flex against her hand as it hardened. Matt's body arched toward her as if encouraging her to continue.

She grasped his phallus in her hand, leaned her head down, and began placing light kisses across his chest.

Suddenly, Matt's body became rigid. "Trudy? What are you doing in here?"

"I was lonely," she said, continuing to kiss him.

"I thought we decided… that we would take things…." Trudy bit down on his nipple. "Ah," he gasped. "Slow."

Trudy changed directions, her trail of kisses moving further down. She flicked her tongue inside his naval, causing

Matt's body to jerk in reaction. "Do you want me to stop now?" she asked seductively.

"Yes," Matt grabbed a handful of her hair. But instead of pulling her away, he urged her head down further.

Trudy slipped her head from his grasp and climbed on top of him, straddling his waist. "I don't understand," she teased. "Was that a yes, or no?"

Matt reached down and grasped her hips, thrusting deep inside her. "No, Trudy. Don't stop. I don't want you to stop."

When Trudy reached her hand across the bed, she found a body there, and this time, it was the person she expected.

She was surprised she had fallen back asleep after having slept away the better part of yesterday. But the fact that they had spent most of the night making love may have had something to do with it.

Matt was already awake and scrolling through his phone, checking messages.

"Mm," purred Trudy as she stretched, feeling thoroughly satiated.

"You know, that can't happen again," said Matt, looking up from his phone.

"*What* can't happen?"

"Last night can't happen again," Matt answered.

"Why?" asked Trudy. "We're two consenting adults."

"It has undone all the progress we've made."

Trudy eyed him warily. "What progress?"

"Of taking things slow. Getting to know each other."

"Yeah, I can see what you mean. It's been what, two days? I think the only thing I've gotten to know about you is how secretive you are." Trudy remarked.

"And, how good I am in bed," Matt added, donning a mischievous grin.

Trudy cut her eyes at him and continued. "I think you know everything there is to know about me. Whenever you're ready to open up, I'm ready." Trudy laid her head onto her palm and stared at him.

"Maybe later." Matt pulled the covers back and got out of bed. "I need to get to the office."

"And, I guess, I'll make myself busy around here?" Trudy asked flippantly.

"Don't forget, I'm going to need your resumé," said Matt as he closed the bathroom door behind him.

"No problem," said Trudy to the door.

She supposed she could use a shower herself. Trudy picked her dress off the floor on the way back to her room.

After putting away the clothes from the day before, Trudy walked to the end of the bed and fell back, her arms spread out behind her. She peered at the ceiling as if it held the answers she was seeking.

I miss Eric, she thought. And Blue. And Cori, if she was being honest.

Before Matt had come back into her life, it had started to become monotonous and routine. She had wished for a change. Huh, guess you should be careful what you wish for, because the place in her life was in right now, was depressing.

If she were back at home, she would have just gotten the kids off to school, and she would be getting ready for work. At home, she had Eric, who loved her, and Shawna. No, she didn't have Shawna anymore. Trudy felt a tear roll down the side of her face.

She had thought she felt alone before, but here not only was she alone, she was lonely. Trudy had come to Texas to be with Matt, but all he did was push her away.

She sat up. Enough musing over the things she could not control. She would focus on what she could. Matt would need her resumé, and she would start on it once she'd bathed, got dressed, and had her morning coffee. But first, she would call Eric's cell and leave him a message.

A knock at the door startled her. Matt poked his head in before giving her a chance to answer.

"I'm getting ready to head out. If you need anything," Matt reached into his suit jacket and pulled out his wallet. "I'm leaving my credit card here." He held the card out to her. When she didn't move, he tossed it on the bed beside her.

"I know at the current moment you are a lady of leisure, but you *are* going to bathe and get dressed sometime today, aren't you?"

Trudy looked down at herself. She was only wearing her bra and panties. "Yes," Trudy said simply. She didn't feel as if she owed him an explanation.

"Well, okay," said Matt, as if he wasn't sure if he should believe her or not. "Don't forget, I'm going to need that resumé."

"Already on it," Trudy responded, holding up her thumb.

"Do you need access to a computer?"

"Nope. Brought my laptop with me."

"Okay. The Wi-Fi is KellyM, and the password is 1Enterprise. The number one and a capital E." Matt was silent for a second. "Do you need to write that down?"

"Got it. All up here." Trudy tapped the side of her head.

Matt narrowed his eyes. "Are you okay? You seem a bit… off."

Trudy took a deep breath. She knew she was being difficult. "I'm fine. Just tired of sitting around all day doing nothing. I guess I'm not cut out for the life *of a woman of leisure.*"

"I'll try to get back here for lunch, but if I can't, I'll call to let you know." Matt walked over and kissed her on her forehead. "See you later," he said before leaving.

Trudy picked up her phone from the nightstand and turned it on. She watched the screen light up as she listened to the front door close.

A few seconds later, she noted the stream of messages as they flooded across her screen. Most of them were from James. She had several voicemails and a message from Eric that said, 'Hey.'

Trudy tapped on James's messages and scanned them for words like Cori, Eric, or Blue in case there was anything serious that she needed to worry about. The only words that stood out were 'divorce' and 'attorney.'

She messaged James back, saying she would contact him in a few days. Trudy called Eric next. She was expecting it to go to voicemail, but he answered on the second ring.

"Hey, Mom."

"Hi, Eric," said Trudy.

"When are you coming back?" Eric asked.

"I'm not sure. Why aren't you in school?"

"Dad let me stay home today."

Trudy was suddenly on alert. "What's wrong? Everything okay?"

"I just didn't feel like going," he responded pensively.

"Why? Something happen at school?"

"No. Just missing my mom."

Trudy placed the call on mute and laid her head in a pillow to muffle her cry.

"Mom, are you still there?" Eric's voice called through the phone.

She took a deep breath before answering. "Yes, baby. I'm here. I just needed a moment. I miss you too, Eric."

"Why did you leave?"

"I needed some time away. Sometimes adults need breaks."

"Like when you went to see your friend Beverly?"

"Yes, like when I went to see Beverly."

"So, you'll be back soon?" Eric asked eagerly.

Trudy paused for a second. She had planned to explain all this in her voicemail. She wasn't prepared to have this conversation. "I'm not sure how long I'll be gone this time. But when I get settled, I'll be back to see you."

"For good? You'll be home for good?"

"No, I don't think so." Trudy wasn't certain if things would work out here with Matt, but even if they didn't, she was sure that she and James would never be husband and wife again. "Maybe once I'm settled, you can come and live with me."

"I guess that means you and Dad are getting a divorce then?

"I think so," Trudy answered quietly.

"I've heard him on the phone talking about it." Eric confided. "I would like to live with you, but I don't think Dad's gonna let me."

"We'll see."

"He did say he misses you."

Trudy didn't know how to respond, so she changed the

subject. "I've got some work to do here today that I need to get started on. Can I call you back later?"

"Okay. Is it alright if I tell Dad I talked to you?"

"Yes. I don't want you keeping secrets from your dad. I know I snuck off in the middle of the night without saying a word, but don't be like me. That was wrong. Okay?"

"Okay," answered Eric.

"By the way, how is Blue?"

"He's fine," he said. "Cori and I are taking turns walking him and making sure he eats."

"That's good," said Trudy, smiling to herself. She had felt bad that she had to leave Blue behind, but she was glad that the kids had stepped up and were taking care of of him. "I have to go now, but remember, I love you."

"Me too, Mom."

"Later."

"Later," said Eric before ending the call.

Trudy ran another bubble bath. A cold shower would have been better, but she hoped a soak in the tub would work the second time around and help settle her nerves. She was starting to think that her decision to jump on a plane to Texas had not been well thought out.

With her being over a thousand miles away, how was she planning on seeing the kids regularly? What would custody look like? Cori would be turning eighteen in less than a year, so seeing her would not be an issue—if she would even consider it.

But what if James kept Eric from her out of spite? She had never known him to be malicious, but divorce could bring out pretty nasty temperaments in some people. Especially those who had been hurt and felt they had been wronged.

Although she had been a coward and skulked away in the middle of the night, Trudy had not touched the bank accounts, even though most of the money in them had been from her paychecks. That should count for something, shouldn't it?

She had every intention of continuing to support the household from Texas. At least until enough time had passed during their separation for things to seem normal. But the fact that she was not currently earning an income was going to make that impossible.

The bubble bath wasn't helping. The lavender-scented bath bombs were having no effect, as thoughts continued to race through her mind. And although she had no actual plans for the rest of the day, getting Matt that resumé was nagging away at her.

Trudy grabbed the sides of the bathtub, stood up too quickly, and spilled water over the sides. "Ugh," she groaned. Now she would have to spend time she could be doing something else, cleaning water off the floor, and she hadn't even had her coffee yet.

Twenty-five minutes later, Trudy was sitting in the kitchen, staring at her resumé on her laptop. For the most part, it was up to date. She had reformatted the document a few months ago to make sure it was current, when she'd first considered getting a second job.

The only thing she needed to do now, was replace the word *Present* in her record of employment with the hardware store, with an end date. Although the decision to leave her husband and kids a few days ago had been a difficult one, she loved her kids and, at one time, had loved James too, but she had also loved her job. The idea of putting an end date terrified Trudy. Adding those ten characters felt like a place of no return.

Maybe it was because Mr. Dalsin had allowed her the option to come back. You know what, she didn't have to add an end date. People submitted resumés all the time while they were still working at another job. Besides, she was giving it directly to Matt, and he owned the company.

Now that was settled, what did she do with it? Trudy didn't have Matt's email address to send it to him, and she did not see a printer lying around anywhere.

She tried searching for a device on her laptop, but nothing came up. If Matt had a printer, it wasn't turned on.

Trudy could try submitting it through the company's website, but first, she would text Matt to see if he wanted it sent digitally or handed to him on paper. She tried calling his cell. Voicemail. She sent a text. 'Resumé is done. How do I get it to you?' Send.

Placing her elbows on top of the kitchen island, she leaned forward, laying her cheeks on her fist, and looked around the apartment.

Now what?

Maybe starting a journal? Trudy read somewhere that it could be therapeutic. She opened a blank document on her computer and stared at the flashing cursor. After a few minutes she placed her fingers on the keyboard and began to type.

> *I am a hot mess. I am a terrible*
> *person who left her family to run off*
> *and have mind-blowing sex with a man who...*

Trudy backspaced, deleting the words. Who...what, no longer desired her? Last night dispelled that. She started again. Maybe something positive this time.

Today, I am bored out of my mind.
Trying to think of words to write in
a journal that has been unsuccessful
thus far.

She closed her laptop. Perhaps the building had a gym. Trudy called down to the front desk.

"Alivia Towers, this is Jerry. How may I help you?"

"Hi, Jerry. Trudy from the fifteenth floor. Is there a workout area in the building?"

"Yes, ma'am. It is located in the lobby, past the front desk. However, it does require a key to get in, but I can grant you access."

"Thank you. I will be down in about ten minutes."

"See you then."

Trudy quickly changed out of her clothes and tossed on a pair of grey stretch capris and a white T-shirt, which she had hastily thrown into her suitcase when she was packing. Unfortunately, she had forgotten socks. She would just have to wear her shoes without them.

Jerry was standing near the front desk when the elevator doors opened. He nodded at Trudy and began walking, leading her down a long corridor she had never noticed before.

At the end was a door labeled Spa, with a small window that revealed a workout area. Jerry pulled a key card out of his pocket and waved it across a keypad. A green light flashed as the door made a buzzing sound.

He opened the door and stood back, allowing Trudy to enter. "Enjoy your workout."

Needing Jerry to open every door for her was starting to

get a bit old. Although he never showed any irritation in having to accommodate her throughout the day, it must be starting to wear thin on him as well. "Thank you." Trudy smiled awkwardly. "I will have to see about getting that key."

Jerry nodded and walked away.

Talk about amenities. The gym appeared to have every workout equipment known to man, and there were three of everything. The treadmills and stationary bikes allowed the user to stream live workouts. Near the back were his and her saunas, showers, and another door labeled Pool. 50-inch TVs were mounted on the walls, and loud music played from speakers placed in the ceiling.

As she was about to step onto a treadmill, Trudy realized she had not brought a water bottle. She scanned the room and saw a refrigerator with sliding glass doors set against one of the walls. It was stocked with water, protein drinks, and fruit juices. On a table beside the refrigerator were stacks of folded towels. Trudy selected a twenty-ounce bottle of water, a hand towel and returned to the treadmill.

She placed her earbuds into her ears, turned on the treadmill, and gradually moved the dial up to a comfortable speed. After running for about five minutes, Trudy was panting and out of breath. She placed her feet on the foot rails while she decreased the belts to a walking speed.

Here, she had thought that her daily walks with Blue had made her into some sort of athlete. Nope, she was out of shape. Trudy gulped down the bottle of water in between breaths and left a few ounces to pour on top of her head. She walked for a few more minutes, then got off. She was done for the day.

Checking her phone before leaving the gym, she saw that there were no messages from Matt.

Jerry let Trudy back into the apartment. She made a mental note to ask Matt for a key when he came in today. She took a quick shower and rechecked her phone after getting dressed. Still no message.

Trudy sat down at her laptop, found Kelly Enterprise's website, clicked on the link to their career page, and began looking at the available positions. She searched through the job postings, but there were not any for Payroll or Accounting. However, there was a section to create a profile and upload a resumé to be considered for future job openings.

Trudy completed the profile information and clicked next. On the following page, she was directed to upload her resumé. She was searching through her documents when her phone rang. It was Matt.

"Hey," said Trudy.

"Hey. I was calling to tell you to go ahead and print out a copy of your resumé. There is a printer in my room. I don't use it often, so it's most likely turned off. Once you print it out, I'll bring it with me to the office tomorrow."

Trudy began exiting the website. "Will you be here for lunch?"

"No, doesn't look like I'll be able to make it back before the end of the day. You understand, right?"

"Sure," Trudy responded dismissively. "So, um…when you called, I was on your company's website, and I didn't see any positions in Payroll or Accounting."

"Well, no. If we were to post the position, then that would mean we would have to sort through applicants. And what would be the point, when I had already planned to give the job to you?"

Trudy supposed that made sense. But he had not even asked for her resumé until that encounter with Brian at the restaurant.

"Okay, yeah, that makes sense."

"Is everything okay?" asked Matt.

"Everything's fine. I was just thinking…Well, you know what they say about idle minds."

"The good news is you have this big city to explore. Call down and have Jerry order you a car for the day. Maybe see if Robert is available. You and he seem to have hit it off. Treat yourself to lunch and maybe some more shopping."

"Maybe. But, it would be nice if I had someone else to do it with."

"What do you mean? Robert will be there."

Trudy was about to respond that she had meant *him*, but Matt was interrupted by someone in the background. "Sorry, Mr. Kelly, but that phone call you were expecting is on the line."

"Thank you, Angela. Sorry, Trudy, I have to go. Enjoy your day."

Trudy walked over to the drawer that contained the to-go menus.

Looks like lunch will be dine-in today.

After calling in her lunch order, Trudy sat back down at her computer and opened another blank document. Maybe she could try that diary again.

CHAPTER 11

I T HAD BEEN three days since Trudy gave Matt her resumé, and he still had not invited her to the office.

She was in her bedroom, repacking her suitcase and brainstorming the best way to ask Matt for money, to buy a plane ticket home. If he were willing to give her the money, Trudy's next decision would be to figure out where she would be staying once the plane landed. There was a chance she could return home. She had never actually told James she had left him for another man. But even if he were to take her back, there was no way things could go back to how they were before. What would their living arrangements look like? The house had only three bedrooms. She supposed the living room couch would have to do.

If push came to shove, there was a little over five thousand dollars left in her 401k, after she rolled part of the money over into an IRA a few months ago. Trudy could call the investment company to see about making a withdrawal, and use some of it to purchase a ticket and a hotel for a few days.

She was placing a few of her clothes that Matt had sent out to be laundered in her suitcase, when he knocked on her door. "Come in," Trudy answered.

"What are you doing?" Matt asked.

"Just putting away laundry."

"Looks to me like you're packing."

Trudy shrugged her shoulders.

"Well, I hope you left something out to wear to the office? Robert should be by around 12:30 to pick you up."

Trudy stood frozen, holding a blouse in her hands mid-air. Had she heard him correctly? She was actually going to work today. "Sure, sure. I have the perfect outfit already picked out."

"I guess I'll see you around 1?" Matt withdrew his head and left.

Trudy began taking all the clothes out of the suitcase and putting them back into the dresser drawers.It looks like things were starting to turn around. She and Matt still weren't sleeping with each other—well, not since the one time—and sitting on opposite sides of the couch when they watched a movie together, but at least the job was real.

Robert was already waiting for Trudy in the lobby when she came downstairs. They walked out to the car together, and she waited while he opened the door for her. Once they were inside, and Robert placed his seat belt on, he turned to her. "I hope you are feeling better today?"

Trudy knew he was alluding to the incident a few days ago after she'd had too much to drink. Although the question could be taken in several different ways, from concern to contempt, she didn't think he intended it to be malicious.

"I am doing well today," she smiled. "In fact, it's my first day starting a new job."

"Oh. Well, congratulations are in order. Best wishes on

your new position."

"Thank you, Robert," Trudy responded graciously.

"What type of job is it? I imagine if it involves a car and driver, it must be something important."

The smile Trudy wore faltered a fraction of an inch. She had no idea what position she would be filling. Matt had not gone into any details, and she had not thought to ask. "Just boring stuff, dealing with numbers," she shook her head dismissively. "How long have you been at your job?"

"Me?" Robert asked, taking one hand off the steering wheel to point at his chest. "I've been driving going on twelve years now."

"Does it ever get monotonous? I could not imagine being cooped up in a car for most of the day. I nearly went crazy on the plane ride here."

"Well, I could never imagine staring at numbers all day." Robert laughed jokingly. "But, no, I love it. Every day, there is something different, and I get to meet new people." Robert glanced at Trudy in the rearview mirror. "Although, most people I pick up aren't trying to have a conversation with the *driver*. But, you could never imagine what you can learn about people when you are stuck in traffic together."

Trudy peered out the window at the road ahead, searching for any deterrents. "You don't expect any today, do you?"

"There isn't any construction on our route, and most of the rush hour traffic has passed, so we should make it on time."

The time on Trudy's phone read 12:40. "And how much longer until we reach our destination?"

"In about eight minutes. Don't worry. I'm like the post office. My delivery rate is about ninety-eight percent."

Trudy sat back against the cushioned leather upholstered

seats. She didn't know why, but she was feeling anxious. Even if she were late, Matt had been the one to send Robert. He would understand, wouldn't he? He wouldn't fire her for being late on her first day.

Trudy thought she had felt unsettled over the last few years of her marriage, but that type of uncertainty was familiar territory. Here, everything was unknown, and she did not have a grasp on any of it.

Within a few minutes, the car pulled in front of the tower-like building that Trudy had only seen pictures of, and Robert was at her door, letting her out.

He tipped his hat and said good luck as he left her standing on the sidewalk, nervously twisting the strap of her purse in her hands.

Trudy took several breaths. "Okay," she said to herself. "New is good."

It's only a building full of people just like you. And sleeping with the boss doesn't give you any special treatment. If you're late, you'll make a bad impression. Get going.

Somehow, Trudy put one foot in front of the other and made her way inside the building to the receptionist's desk.

The woman behind the desk looked up when Trudy neared. "Hello. How may I help you?"

Trudy swallowed. "Trudy Allen. Here to see Mr. Kelly."

The woman began swiping through a tablet. "Yes, I see your name here. Can you take a seat?" she said, motioning to a seating area behind Trudy. "I'll let someone know you're here."

Trudy found a seat and immediately became apprehensive when she noticed the few other people waiting were carrying either a briefcase or satchel. She had only thought to bring her purse and cellphone.

She didn't have too much time to question her decision before the receptionist called out to her, "Ms. Allen, they are ready for you now."

Trudy stood up and looked around, expecting to see Matt coming out to greet her, but no one was there.

"Just take the elevators to your left to the twelfth floor, and let the receptionist know you are here to see Mr. Kelly."

As she walked to the elevators indicated by the receptionist, Trudy felt her heart racing in her chest. She pushed the button labeled up and focused on the arrow as she tried to will her heart to settle down.

The elevator doors opened. Directly in front of her was another desk. Before Trudy could let the receptionists know why she was there, one of them, a young man in his early twenties with dark brown hair, wearing slacks and a dark blue vest over a cream dress shirt, was already coming from behind the desk to greet her.

"Hi, Ms. Allen. I hope the trip up was not too unpleasant."

Trudy noted that he appeared overly excited to see her, or maybe it was just his usual demeanor. She wasn't sure.

"No, not at all," Trudy said, shaking her head. "Although, it is a bit hot up here." She wiped the back of her palm across her forehead.

"Oh, is it?" he said, tilting his head to one side. "I hadn't noticed. My name is Tyler, and I will be helping you get situated today. If you'll follow me."

As Trudy followed Tyler, they passed several people sitting in cubicles, talking into earpieces. A few of them stopped conversing long enough to acknowledge her with a nod and then continued their conversations.

On her left was a conference room with glass paneling. About ten people were seated around a table, and Trudy could see Matt standing at the head.

Tyler walked at a steady pace as he pointed out several different areas located on the floor. Trudy barely heard anything he said. She could now feel her heart beating in her throat, and she found it hard to catch her breath. It was as if she were on the treadmill again, and she could feel perspiration on her forehead.

Tyler stopped in front of a small office and motioned toward the entrance. "And this is your office."

Trudy gingerly took a few steps inside, then collapsed on the floor. She began to pant, taking deep breaths in and out, but regardless of how much air she took in, it did not seem like it was enough. It felt like a weight was bearing down on her chest, and the coffee she'd had this morning was threatening its way back up.

She thought she could hear Tyler speaking to her, but she wasn't sure. There was a thick pounding in her ears, overwhelming her senses. She *was* able to feel the hand pressing on the back of her neck, which she eventually gave in to, allowing it to push her head forward as she pulled her knees to her.

"Breathe. Okay? Just breathe." Tyler chanted.

By the time Trudy got her breathing under control, she looked up and found that a small crowd had formed outside her office. She quickly placed her head back between her knees, hiding her face from the onlookers.

There was a tap on her shoulder. She looked up to see an attractive woman, a few years younger than her, with shoulder-length red hair and a heart-shaped face, smiling down at her.

"Hi, Trudy. I'm Gabby, the in-house nurse practitioner. Do you mind if I take a look to see how you're doing?"

Trudy timidly nodded her head.

"Okay." Gabby kneeled beside her as she placed a stethoscope in her ears. "I'm going to listen to your heart." Gabby placed the diaphragm on Trudy's chest. "It's beating a little quick, but it sounds good. Have you eaten today?"

Trudy nodded again.

"What did you have to eat?" Gabby placed the diaphragm on Trudy's back.

"A cup of coffee."

"Can you take a deep breath?"

Trudy breathed in through her nose and held her breath for a few seconds before letting it out.

"Is that your normal breakfast?" asked Gabby.

"Yes," Trudy answered.

"You really should try to eat something." Gabby stood up and placed her stethoscope inside her medical bag. "I think you'll be okay. I think you may have experienced a panic attack. Tyler," she said, turning to the receptionist. "Can you bring her some water and some cashews?"

"On it." Tyler scurried from the office. His path unhampered now that the small crowd had lost interest after hearing Trudy had only suffered a panic attack.

Gabby reached her hand out to Trudy. "Can I help you up?"

It took Trudy a few seconds to realize she was sitting on the floor. She could feel her cheeks growing warm. She gave Gabby a small smile and reached up and took the hand that was offered.

"Thank you," Trudy said after making sure she was able to stand without assistance. She then tucked her blouse back into the waistband of her pants. "I guess I've made an impression on my first day."

"Don't worry. They won't talk about you too long." Gabby teased.

"How long is too long?" asked Trudy, eyeing her warily.

"Don't worry about it. First days can be stressful. And I'm sure someone here will throw some sort of temper tantrum before the day's out, that will overshadow this small little incident."

"Temper tantrum?" Trudy raised an eyebrow. "Really?"

"*Really*. The stress levels around here are through the roof. Why do you think they have their own in-house practitioner?" Gabby asked, raising an eyebrow as well.

"I appreciate you coming to look in on me," said Trudy.

"Like I said, it's my job. And since you appear to be doing better, I will leave you to yours." Gabby turned to leave.

"Thanks again."

Gabby hesitated at the door, then turned back to face Trudy. "If you need someone to talk to, my number and email are in the office directory."

Trudy smiled. "I may take you up on that."

The rest of the day went without incident, so much so that Trudy was bored out of her mind. Most of her work consisted of performing internal audits of the company's previous year's financial records.

Whoever had been in charge of maintaining the records had done an impeccable job. Every penny was accounted for.

Along with the water and cashews, Tyler had returned to Trudy's office with a stack of files and a message.

"I have a bit of bad news," Tyler said, scrunching up his face. "Turns out that because you are not certified as a CPA in the state of Texas, you won't be allowed to work at the company in an 'official capacity,'" he said, using air quotes.

Ergo, she would be doing grunt work.

"But," he said, trying to sound chipper. "The company will give you time to study for the exam and pay for any expenses towards your certificate."

Trudy threw back her head and gave out a loud sigh. She had dreaded the certification process the first time around, but it had been worth it in the end. And if she had to endure it once again to be trusted with more important work, she would.

"Whatever it takes," she said.

"Sorry," Tyler said, forming his mouth into a pout. "But, if there's nothing else?"

"No. Thank you, Tyler." Trudy pursed her lips together. "There's nothing else."

"You know where to find me if you need me," he said, flaring his hands out dramatically in front of him before spinning around and taking his leave.

She had spent most of the day in her office hiding, too embarrassed to face anyone, although the glass walls made it impossible. Trudy could have closed the blinds, but she had not wanted to draw any more attention to herself. But now she was experiencing a more pressing matter: her bladder was full.

From her sightline, it appeared that the foot traffic outside her office had died down. Either everyone was at their desks, on a break, or gone for the day, making it the perfect time for her to take a break.

Outside her office, there were a few people that she had not been able to see from her desk. One woman looked up as

Trudy passed by. She wore an expectant look on her face as if she had been keeping an eye out to see when Trudy would manifest from her sanctuary.

After finally finding the bathroom, she went to the breakroom in search of something to eat. Lucky for her, it was empty.

Situated in the middle of the breakroom, were several square tables with two wooden back chairs placed at each one. Cushioned booths were fixed against the back wall, and a sliding glass door led to a balcony. On the balcony, were a few picnic tables with umbrellas in the center to block out the sun. Although Trudy would love to get outside and take in some fresh air, she decided against it, seeing that they *were* on the twelfth floor.

On the counter were two single-serve coffee machines, an espresso maker, and three boxes of donuts. Trudy popped in a coffee pod in one of the machines and picked out a flavored creamer while the water heated.

Trudy was trying to decide between a curler or lemon-filled donut when a voice startled her from behind.

"I would recommend the blueberry. If there are any left."

Trudy turned to see Matt. He was staring as if he'd been watching her for a while.

"I really shouldn't have any. Too fattening." She gave him a small smile.

"Knowing you, it will probably be the only thing you've eaten today. Besides, I'm sure one donut wouldn't hurt." Matt said as his eyes trailed down her frame suggestively.

There was that look that Trudy had grown accustomed to. She felt her cheeks redden for the second time today. Back at the apartment, Matt treated her as no more than a guest, but here at work, he was flirting with her. The man was certainly an enigma.

However, with the way he was looking at her now and the way her body was responding, Trudy knew she would be more than willing, to let him take her right there in the middle of the breakroom, if it were not for the fact that someone could walk in any minute.

"It's starting to get a bit warm in here," Trudy said, fanning herself.

Matt's face filled with concern. "I heard about the incident earlier. Are you okay? Gabby said it was a simple panic attack, but do you need me to call her?" Matt asked, moving toward the phone on the breakroom wall.

"No. No, I'm fine." Trudy hurried to reassure him. "I'm not that kind of hot." She averted her eyes. "It's the way you were looking at me."

"Oh. Ooh." Matt said again as he realized what she meant. "I'm sorry. I hadn't realized…but, you're right, it *was* a bit inappropriate for the workplace.

"No problem," Trudy said, moving towards Matt. Feeling a little bold. "As long as you bring a little of it back to the apartment with you later."

Trudy was only a few inches from Matt when Tyler walked into the breakroom. "Trudy. There you are."

Matt jumped back as if he'd been burned. "Yes. She was… is taking a break."

Tyler looked at the two of them questioningly but shook his head as if dismissing his thoughts.

"Well, I was coming in to check on you and report back to Mr. Kelly. But I guess there is no need to now." Tyler crossed one arm in front of him, placing the other on top, before resting his chin in his hand.

It seemed to take Matt a few seconds to realize that Tyler

was waiting for a response. "No, Tyler. There's no need. Ms. Allen and I were just discussing how her first day was going. But, Tyler, now that you are here, I need something else from you. And we can allow Ms. Allen to finish her break."

Matt and Tyler left the breakroom, leaving Trudy alone.

Trudy grabbed her coffee and a curler to take back with her to her office. She wasn't sure how long the breakroom would remain empty. She was still embarrassed and was not ready to exchange pleasantries with anyone who might come in.

When she returned to her office, she saw that Tyler had placed another stack of files on her desk. Trudy checked the clock on the wall. It was now 4:32.

What time did the workday end?

Trudy picked up the office phone to call Tyler but noticed there was a message on her cellphone. Matt had texted to say that Robert would be there at five to pick her up, and he would be staying late. She replaced the phone in its cradle then grabbed her cell phone and purse and looked around the office one last time before heading out.

Jerry was there to greet her when she returned to the apartment that evening. His usual demure behavior had been replaced with a cheerful one, and he was doing a poor job of trying to hide it. "Good evening."

"Evening," Trudy replied, eyeing him curiously. She wondered what he was in such high spirits about, and why he had not moved towards the elevators to take her upstairs. "Will Andrew be taking me up today?" Trudy looked outside to the doorman, who was helping an older woman out of her car.

"No. Today, that honor belongs to you." Jerry, who had been standing with both hands behind his back, suddenly produced a key as if he were performing a magic trick.

Trudy held out her hand to take the key. "Thank you so much. I know you must be as happy as I am."

"What do you mean?" Jerry asked, feigning naivety.

Trudy could see that he was not going to admit he was glad that he was no longer responsible for having to let her into the apartment, so she thanked him once again and used the key to let herself onto the elevator.

The inside of the apartment felt cold and deserted. Trudy craved the sounds of a full house. She missed coming home to Eric shouting at the TV as he sat on the couch playing a video game. Yelling so loud, as he tried to hear himself over the noise of the gaming headset he was wearing. And there had always been Blue to greet her.

The empty apartment stirred up memories of home, and home reminded her of James. It was time to have that uncomfortable conversation she had been putting off. It was time to call him.

Trudy dialed the home number, hoping Eric would pick up and tell her his dad wasn't in yet.

"Trudy?" It was James.

She paused for a second. "Hi, James."

"Didn't think you were going to call."

"Sorry it took me so long."

"So, does this call mean you're coming back?" asked James.

"No," she whispered.

"No? I don't understand. Where are you? Aside from the note you left, you just left here without saying anything. You couldn't talk to me before doing something like this? Is this some kind of ploy for attention?"

Trudy wanted to yell. 'Talk to you? Talk to you! That's

all I've been trying to do for two years now!' But instead, she took a deep breath and replied. "I'm in Texas. I found a job here, and I am planning to continue to contribute to the household, while we figure things out."

"So, you're not coming back?" James spoke so low Trudy barely heard him. "Why Texas, Trudy?" he asked, this time louder, demanding.

"Why not Texas? It's as good a place as any?"

"Well, first of all, as far as I know, you don't know anyone in Texas." James snapped.

"I ran into an old friend a while back. Who offered me a job here."

"Another old friend, huh?" James spat. "And did this *old friend* also offer you a place to live?"

"Yes."

"And how long has this old friend and you been in touch?"

"Not long," Trudy answered warily.

"Evidently, long enough for you to decide it was a good idea to up and leave your family in the middle of the night."

"It's not like that. This is something I have been—"

"Really, Trudy? Do you think I'm stupid? I know it's another man."

"What?" She started. "What gives you that idea?"

"Because, Trudy. I know you. If there were an 'old friend,' you would have told me. You tell me everything. Whether I want to hear it or not," James remarked sarcastically.

Trudy remained silent. She did not know how to respond, too fearful to confirm or deny his accusation.

"Who is it?" James insisted.

"An old work colleague," she mumbled.

"And this job, does it actually exist? Or are you planning

on supporting this family using the money he gives you?"

"Yes, there is a job." Trudy began slowly. "I'm working at his company."

"So, the money *is* from him."

"James, it's not like that!" Trudy exclaimed, feeling attacked.

"Isn't it?" he lashed out. "Look, Trudy, you've had your fun. Okay, I admit I have some responsibility in all of this. I haven't been the husband that you've needed. Just come home. We can work it out. We can go to counseling or something."

"How's Cori?" Trudy asked, changing the subject.

"Cori? Cori's fine. I mean, she refuses to acknowledge she even has a mother and bites Eric's head off if he even mentions you. But other than that, she's fine. If you really want to find out how she's doing, you can come home. Even if she doesn't act like it, Cori needs her mother. We all need you."

A stream of tears began running down her face. Trudy wiped them away absentmindedly. "I'll think about it. Okay? Just give me a few days."

There was a long pause from the other end. "James, are you still there?" Trudy pulled the phone from her ear to check their connection.

"Okay, Trudy," James responded. "But don't take too long. We won't wait forever."

When Trudy woke the next morning, she found Matt lying beside her. He had come in the night before and climbed into the bed, snuggling up to her.

Although it was a Friday night, Trudy had gone to bed

early. The constant thoughts weighing in about James's offer for her to come home and work on their marriage, after knowing she had left him for another man, missing the kids, and the feelings she had developed for Matt, had become too much.

Unfortunately, even after lying down, her mind had not allowed her to fall asleep.

At first, she had pretended to be asleep when she heard him whispering her name at the bedroom door. Trudy assumed that Matt was only there to talk about work and would go away once he saw her still figure lying in the bed. She had been surprised when he had come inside the room and began undressing. Her sharp intake of breath betrayed her when he pulled her close to his naked body.

Trudy had wanted to deny him. Now that James knew about Matt, it felt wrong, and she was starting to experience some of the same guilt she'd felt the first time she had slept with him. But when Matt began kissing the back of her neck, sending shocks of tremors throughout her whole body—

"Mm. You looked so sexy today. I wanted to take you right there in the breakroom," he had said, moaning against her ear—all thoughts of resistance had been erased.

Trudy turned to Matt, wrapping her legs around his waist. "Take me now," she had said. "Take me now."

Trudy lay in bed longer than usual. Sometime during the night, Matt had thrown his arm over her, and she was scared she would wake him if she moved.

Although she would not be going to the office today, she needed to get to her laptop and sign up for a course to prep for her CPA exam.

It's now or never, Trudy thought as she slid out from under Matt's arm, grabbed her robe, and headed off to the kitchen for a cup of coffee.

She was trying to decide between two online courses when Matt walked into the kitchen and grabbed an orange out of the fruit bowl. "It's Saturday. Why are you on the computer?"

"I have to get my certificate to practice in Texas. Remember?"

"That can wait. You're getting paid the same salary as if you were anyway."

Trudy looked up from her laptop, narrowing her eyes. "And no one is questioning that?"

"It's my company. *Remember*?"

"Regardless," she said, looking back at the computer's screen. "I am going to run out of files to review. I will actually have to do some *real* work, sometime."

"But not today." Matt walked over and closed Trudy's laptop. "Come back to bed. It's Saturday."

Last night Trudy had been vulnerable and needed some form of solace, so she had given herself to Matt, but in the light of day, things were different. She recalled how cold and distant he had been since her arrival, and she wasn't sure what had initiated the change at the office and then again last night—leaving her even more hesitant to accept it at face value.

"Maybe later." Trudy gave him a small smile. "I'm going to need a break to recover from last night."

"No problem. We've got the rest of the weekend," said Matt, tossing the orange in the air and catching it.

Trudy stared at him questioningly. "The rest of the weekend? Don't you have to go into the office or something?"

"Not really. I figured you and I could explore the city."

"This city?" asked Trudy, pointing her finger, confused.

"Yes," Matt answered hesitantly.

"You sure you don't want to go somewhere on the outskirts of town, or in the middle of nowhere?"

"No, I mean *this* city. We could get a car or walk. Whichever you want."

"Sure, we could do that," Trudy responded.

Part of her wanted to call him out on his past behavior, but she decided against it. What would be the point? Complaining might cause Matt to resort back to his previous ways, leading him to surmise that there *was* something at the office that needed his attention, and Trudy would be stuck in the apartment by herself again.

"Just let me call and check in on Eric first."

"How are your kids?" Matt asked.

Okay, now things were starting to border on strange Matt had never asked Trudy about her kids before. She hadn't been sure he remembered that she had any. "For the most part, they are doing well," she answered. "All things considered. Thanks for asking."

"You're welcome." Matt waved his hand dismissively before popping an orange slice into his mouth. "I have a few things I need to catch up on. Just let me know when you are ready to head out, and then we can begin our day."

He grabbed another orange as he left the kitchen.

Trudy dialed Eric's cell phone. It went straight to voicemail. *Dang,* she thought. It was around 4 a.m. there.

She kept forgetting the time change. She left a message and ended the call.

There were a few missed calls and emails with the subject

heading 'Call Me Urgent' from Mr. Dalsin on her phone. More than likely about the status of her job. Although Mr. Dalsin had said the job was still hers if she wanted it, he would eventually have to fill the position. She would need to reach out to him soon and let him know she was not coming back.

Trudy laid her phone face down on the countertop and took a few more minutes to finish her coffee, before going back to her room to get ready for her and Matt's outing.

Their first stop was a small bistro near the apartment building. Matt spent most of the walk there raving about the different dishes on the restaurant's brunch menu. Trudy listened to him, pretending to show interest, knowing she had no intention of eating anything.

They chose a table located on the sidewalk outside the restaurant. When the waiter arrived, Matt chose two of his favorite dishes from the menu, French toast, and spinach quiche, along with a cup of orange juice. Trudy ordered a glass of grapefruit juice.

When the food came, he poured a small moat of syrup on his plate, soaking the French toast. "Mm. You really should try some," he said in between mouthfuls.

With every bite, Matt emitted an over-exaggerated note of gratification, causing Trudy to give in and sample a bit of the French toast. He was right. It was delicious. "Are you trying to get me fat?" she asked.

"No," Matt had responded. "It's just food, Trudy. Some of us mere mortals need food to sustain ourselves."

After they finished their meal, they walked to the Modern Art Museum that Trudy had visited when she first came to

Texas. Although she had not found most of the museum pieces to her liking, Trudy found a new appreciation for some of them after Matt described a few of his favorites from his own perspective.

She watched in awe as his face lit up as he pointed out some of the intricate details in the artist's placement of some of their pieces. Trudy still felt that bringing in everyday objects and arranging them in a museum was something anyone could do. It was not the same as creating intricate details by placing brush to canvas, but she supposed people liked what they liked. It was just nice to know that she and Matt had something in common.

Trudy had planned to show Matt 'Eve,' the art display from the exhibit she had fallen in love with, but it had been taken down. The area was now roped off as it lay in wait, to be replaced with another.

Robert was standing by the car when they left the museum. Matt waved him off when he came to the door to open it for Trudy. "I got it this time," Matt said.

Trudy slid over and waited until Matt was beside her. "Where to now?" she asked, full of anticipation.

"I was thinking that we could take a morning cruise of the bayous."

"The bayous?"

"Yeah. It's a lake surrounded by vegetation and wildlife."

"I know what it is. I just didn't know there were any in Texas. Is it dangerous?" she asked, suddenly feeling apprehensive as she considered the type of wildlife they would encounter.

"We will be fine. We will be on a pontoon boat with a

guide and several other passengers. They do thousands of these tours a year. But if you're scared, we can do—"

"No, a mid-morning cruise of the bayou sounds fun," said Trudy, trying to sound convincing.

Riding on a tin boat through a swamp sounded like the least safest pastime in the world. Right now, jumping out of an airplane at ten thousand feet with a surfboard sounded safer. But Matt was trying to make an effort by showing her the city and surprising her with a cruise. Unless all of this was a ploy to get her defenses down so it would be easier to toss her over the side of the boat. Trudy shook her head; she was being silly.

Matt stared at her curiously. "What's on your mind?"

"Nothing. I was just trying to picture what the bayous

of Texas looked like." Yeah, with her lying face down in it, about to be ripped apart by alligators.

"In comparison to what?" asked Matt.

"Huh?" Trudy replied.

"You said you were trying to picture the bayous. Have you been to one before?"

"I've only seen them on TV."

"TV doesn't do it justice. You have to see it for yourself."

"Can't wait," said Trudy, full of fake enthusiasm.

Trudy was sitting in the boat, wearing a life vest, wondering if it was too late to make a break for it. She had tried sitting in the chairs mounted in the middle, but Matt had assured her that they would have a better view from the seats placed on the sides of the boat.

Along with Trudy and Matt, there were eight other passengers, including a family of four, with a young son and toddler. The little girl, who could be no more than three, had a cherub face framed by locks of wispy blond hair, refused to stay in her seat, and kept taking off running around the boat. "I want to see allee-gators," she said.

The little girl reminded Trudy of Cori when she was that age, and could never sit still for more than a minute at a time.

The mother chased after her, catching the little girl up into her arms. Returning to their seats, she plopped her back down. "Be patient, Abigail. You'll see them soon enough."

"Is that allee-gator?" asked Abigail, turning to stand in her seat and leaning out over the rail.

A collective gasp went through the boat.

Her mom grabbed her, pulling her back down. "Sit down, Abigail." She looked around at the other passengers, a disparaging look on her face.

One of the boat's crew members, a young man in his early twenties, posturing with fake bravado, walked over to Abigail's mother. "Ma'am. You're going to have to make sure she's seated the entire time, or we're going to have to ask you to leave."

"I'm sorry. It won't happen again." She looked down at Abigail. "You hear that? If you don't stay in your seat, we won't get to see the alligators. Do you understand?"

"Okay, Mommy," said Abigail. "I be good."

Suddenly, Abigail's father appeared out of nowhere, swooping her up out of her seat and placing the little girl on his lap. "I got it from here," he said to the crew member, who seemed satisfied and walked away.

A daddy's girl. Just like Cori.

Trudy turned away from the family, not wanting to deal with the emotions that had been stirred up inside her from watching them.

A piercing chirping sound emanated from a loudspeaker. "Welcome aboard River Boat cruises. One of the longest-running Pontoon Cruises in Texas." The tour guide announced as the boat pulled away from the dock and began moving through the murky green water.

Trudy gazed out at the lake and shore surrounding them, searching for the nefarious alligators. The only thing she spotted was a giant turtle making its way into the water.

"Look, Abby." The girl's dad pointed out. "A turtle."

"A tur...tle," Abigail repeated. "Look, Davy," Abigail said to her brother. "A tur...tle."

"I see it," said her older brother, unimpressed.

"Are you enjoying yourself?" asked Matt, smoothing Trudy's hair from her face.

"It's nice," she answered.

"Are you sure? You seem tense." Matt tried pulling Trudy close to him.

Her body was so rigid. It took a few seconds before she was able to loosen up and allow herself to be gathered into Matt's embrace. "Sorry, I hadn't realized."

"You could have said no to the cruise," he whispered into her ear.

"I know, but you wanted to show me the city, and I wanted to let you."

"I appreciate that, but it's okay if we don't like the same things. It's not necessary to be compatible in every area of our lives." Matt said as he ran his hand down her inner thigh.

Trudy checked to see if anyone was watching them. Luckily, everyone else had their eyes trained on the swamps. "We can't do this here."

"Okay. I'll stop if you want me to." Matt moaned against her ear.

"You're not being fair. You know I can't resist you when you talk that way."

"In what way?" Matt leaned in closer, brushing his lips against the tender part of her neck.

"Look, allee-gator." Abigail squealed.

Trudy immediately stiffened in her seat. She could hear everyone talking at one time and saw a few people pull out their phones before she closed her eyes shut.

"It's okay." Matt wrapped his arms around her torso. "You're safe. They can't get on the boat, and if they did, the crew members have guns with tranquilizers. Besides, the alligators would most likely go after the little ones first. They're easier to digest."

Trudy swatted Matt's hand. "That's not funny." She giggled as she opened her eyes and saw Abigail trying to reach out over the railing again, and her father catching her back into his lap.

"Better now?" asked Matt.

"Yes. I'm better. Thank you."

"That's what I'm here for."

Trudy was able to keep her eyes open for the rest of the cruise as she became more comfortable in her surroundings. She listened intently as the tour guide pointed out several white-tailed deer, a few armadillos, and a bobcat.

Trudy found it interesting that such docile creatures as deer and rabbits could live among ferocious animals like bobcats and alligators. She became immersed in the history of the bayous as she sat erect, craning to see the animals hiding among the foliage like the other passengers. Still, she was glad when the cruise ended and was able to place her feet on sturdier ground. However, because the dock was located near the water, Trudy still kept a lookout for alligators.

CHAPTER 12

TRUDY SAT IN her office, daydreaming about her and Matt's weekend. After the pontoon cruise, they had gone back to the apartment and ordered in. The rest of their evening was spent in Matt's room, lying in bed and watching old movies. Sunday had been much more of the same. By the end of the weekend, Matt had asked Trudy to move her things into his room, and was even offering to redecorate the guest bedroom so that her kids could use it when they visited.

He was already gone when she woke up this morning. On his pillow were two yellow calla lilies and a note that read. 'See you later. Love Matt.'

She was staring at the lilies that were now in the pencil holder on her desk, when Tyler walked in with two more folders.

"These are the rest of last year's financials. From now on, all information will be sent to you via email. Which means…you no longer get to see this pretty face every two hours?" said Tyler, framing his face with his hands.

"Well, if I find myself missing you," said Trudy. "I'll just poke my head out of my office."

"Yeah. I guess you could do that." Tyler responded, playfully bobbing his head.

Trudy placed a hand on top of the folders. "I'll get to these after my break."

"No hurry." Tyler turned to leave.

Trudy followed Tyler out of her office. He went back to his desk, and she went off in search of coffee.

Most of the tables in the breakroom were full. A few of her co-workers were sitting outside on the balcony, enjoying one of the less-than-sweltering days they had been recently experiencing. Some of them addressed Trudy when she walked in, the awkwardness of her first day already forgotten, and she spoke back.

Gabby had been right; someone else had eventually had a meltdown. It happened on Friday, near the end of the workday. Brian had stormed out of a meeting with Matt, yelling something about business ethics and morals. It had been the first time Trudy had seen him since she started working there, the first time since their encounter at the Mexican restaurant.

Matt had tried to get Brian to come back into his office, but he had refused. "Everyone here should know the kind of man they're working for," Brian said, casting his gaze over the people staring back at him.

Gabby had arrived and was able to get Brian to calm down before taking him back to her office.

When Trudy had asked Matt about it later that night, he had simply told her that Brian was burnt out from working too much and would be taking a short leave of absence. He declined to talk about it any further when Trudy had tried pressing him.

Trudy made herself a cup of coffee and selected a fruit

cup from the refrigerator before going back to her office. On her way, she saw Matt heading into a meeting. He nodded his head in her direction and smiled before going into the conference room.

Inside her office, Trudy took a seat at her desk to eat her lunch. She pulled the lid off the fruit cup and spooned a few of the bite-sized chunks into her mouth.

As she chewed, her gaze was drawn towards the time on her computer. She had fifteen minutes left on her break. She ate another spoonful. This time, her eyes strayed to the last two folders sitting on top of her desk.

There were still four hours left in her workday, and the folders were undoubtedly the only work Trudy would have until then. From the looks of the files, it would most likely only take her about an hour apiece to get through them, leaving her with nothing to do for the rest of the day. Even with her knowing this, it was hard to ignore them.

Trudy needed to make some friends here so she could stop taking lunch in her office, and start hanging out in the breakroom like everyone else. She considered playing a game on her phone, but the files continued to beckon.

She didn't actually have to begin working on them now; she could just flip through them.

Ensuring the area in front of her was clear, Trudy picked up the file lying on top and set it in front of her. It was dated April 3rd of this year and appeared to be an open account for land acquisition. Somehow, Tyler had given her the wrong folder. She'd have to call him back to get it.

As she was closing the cover, an address on the paperwork inside caught her eye: 1641 Forney Ln. Mr. Dalsin's hardware store. Why would Matt's company seek to acquire the land on which the hardware store resided?

Sliding her fruit cup off to the side, Trudy placed her fingertips above her top lip and began kneading the skin there. She sat for a moment, focused on a corner in her office, as answers to so many of her questions began to fall into place. Unconsciously forming her hand into a fist, she placed it against the knot forming in her chest. Suddenly, she wasn't feeling so well.

When Matt came back to town a few months ago, he had tried to buy the hardware store, and Mr. Dalsin turned him down. But instead of leaving, Matt stayed, saying he had other business in town, and ultimately began pursuing her. Her lunch dates with Matt began to arouse suspicion and had caused Mr. Dalsin to question her loyalty to him.

Later, when Trudy asked Matt about his offer to buy the hardware store, Matt explained that it was simply a nice gesture that would provide Mr. Dalsin a reason to retire, never mind the fact that the company was to be passed down to his son.

But, of course, that had been a lie. There had been nothing innocent about his gesture. And Trudy was the accountant, and Matt had needed to keep her close.

Another piece of the puzzle suddenly clicked into place, the fake email that was sent while she was out of town visiting Beverly—her heart sank even further. She had questioned the timing of the email then but soon dismissed it as a coincidence.

The emails marked urgent from Mr. Dalsin. Trudy opened her phone and scrolled until she found the last email.

> *Trudy, do you know anything about a company called Kelly Enterprises? There's a contract for them to buy the land the hardware store is located on, and they are planning to double the rent. I can't*

The email was dated five days ago. Trudy opened the folder and flipped through the pages, praying it wasn't there. But it was. The completion date of the contract was dated this past Friday. The day Brian had returned to the office. The day of his blow-up when he'd questioned Matt about his morals.

Somehow, he must have figured out who Trudy was and how she fit into all this. Too bad she hadn't been able to work it out on her own. She could have saved Mr. Dalsin's company. For all the years she spent in school, earning her degree and working as an accountant, she hadn't been able to put two and two together and see what was right in front of her.

The knot in her chest had grown wider, and tears began pooling in her eyes. Trudy quickly wiped them away. No, she would not do this here. She closed the folder, sat back in her chair, shut her eyes, and took a deep breath.

There was a knock on her door. Trudy slowly raised her eyelids. It was Tyler. "I think I brought you the wrong file."

Trudy picked up the folder and started to hand it to him, but hesitated. "Is Mr. Kelly still in his meeting?"

"I think so." Tyler extended his hand. "Can I get the file?"

"It's for Mr. Kelly, right?"

"Yes, sort of," Tyler responded. "Instead of giving it to you, it was supposed to have gone to Tracy in accounting."

"So, there is an actual Accounting Department?" Trudy scoffed.

"Yes, it's on another floor."

He kept me here to keep an eye on me.

"You know what…I'll make sure Tracy gets it."

"But you've never been on the eleventh floor. Have you?" Tyler eyed her suspiciously.

Trudy got up from her seat and tucked the folder under her arm. "Don't worry, Tyler, I think I can manage."

She straightened her shoulders, lifted her head, and made her way across the office floor. A few employees looked up as Trudy passed by but quickly dismissed her before returning to their phone calls. She stopped when she reached the conference room. Trying the door handle, it turned easily in her hand. She pushed the door open and stepped into the room.

Matt, who was in the middle of a lecture, stopped when he saw her. "Trudy… um…Ms. Allen. What are you doing here?"

"I heard you were looking for this," Trudy said, holding out the folder. "I wanted to make sure I hand-delivered it to you personally."

The other members in the room were casting her curious looks. One person rushed over to the office phone in the corner, probably a special line dedicated to Gabby.

"What folder?" asked Matt.

"The land acquisition file," Trudy said, taking a step towards him. "You know, the land that Dalsin's and Sons hardware store is located on." She moved in closer. "You know Dalsin and Son, right? After all, Mr. Dalsin gave you your first job. And now you are what…trying to steal his company from him? And why...Matt? Because he wouldn't sell it to you?"

Trudy placed the folder on the table in front of him. "How could you?!" she raged, her whole body shaking. "I left my job, my family."

She could feel the tears forming again. No. She wouldn't

cry here. "Never mind, it doesn't matter now." Trudy turned to walk away.

"No one forced you to—"

All the hurt, anger, and frustration wailed up inside her and before she could stop herself, she spun around, wanting to hurt Matt as much as he'd hurt her. She watched as her hand flung out and landed against his jaw.

"Trudy." She heard a voice yell out above the gasps in the conference room.

"Trudy," the voice called out again now from right behind her. "This kind of behavior is unacceptable—"

Trudy swung around to face Gabby. "Right now, I don't care what you think." She spat out between clenched teeth.

Trudy scanned the faces of those in the conference room and the people looking in from the office floor. They were looking at her as if she were a woman gone mad. The walls were starting to feel like they were closing in on her, and she needed to get out of there. She took one last look at Matt and walked out.

"Are you going to just let her leave?" Gabby questioned Matt. "She assaulted you."

"It's fine. Let her go," Matt answered, sounding defeated.

Trudy stood outside the office building, trying to decide which direction to go. Other than the view from her rides to work each morning, she didn't know much about this area of town. But what she did know is, she needed to walk. Because if she didn't keep moving, she would fall, broken, atop the asphalt-covered ground. And after everything else she had allowed herself to be subjected to, she would not give Matt the satisfaction of breaking her.

The streets of the business district were busy for this time of day, but most of the sidewalks were empty, except for a few food vendors that were shutting down their pushcarts. Trudy moved about, mostly in a daze, as she tried to fight back the tears that threatened to consume her.

Eventually, twilight fell, and the once-active area was now dormant and had grown to become immuring and minacious. Trudy could no longer continue to roam about alone. Unfortunately, there was only one place to go: back to Matt's.

Now, how to get there. Trudy walked over to the bus stop and began reading the times on the bus schedule. The next bus was due in twenty minutes. She cast her eyes up to the sky. It would be much darker then. She guessed she should have thought this out. Even if it were safe enough to stand outside alone until a bus came, she couldn't be sure if she'd be waiting on the right bus. Maybe she should be standing at the stop across the street. Also, she had left her phone and purse in the office. She had no way of paying.

Although the office was still open, Trudy dreaded walking back in there and having to face all those people again, but she supposed it would be better than standing out on a street corner. She turned around the way she had come and noticed a car stopped along the street, a few yards away.

As she neared the car, she realized it was familiar. The passenger window rolled down. "Are you okay, Ms. Allen?" asked Robert.

Trudy leaned down so they could be face to face. "Hi, Robert. Yes. I'm okay," she said, not sure if it were true.

"Mr. Kelly called me to look for you. I've been following you for a few blocks now. Are you ready to go home?"

Trudy threw her head back and laughed.

Home, where was that? She had no home.

"Did I say something funny?" Robert questioned, confused.

"No, I'm just a little out of sorts right now. But yes, I am ready to go back to the apartment. But if we could stop by the office first. I left some things there."

"It's already taken care of." Robert opened his door to get out. "Mr. Kelly brought your things to me earlier."

"I've got it," said Trudy, stopping Robert. "I can get my own door today."

Robert nodded and closed his door.

In the back seat were her purse and cellphone. Trudy picked up the phone, intending to call Mr. Dalsin, but set it back down. What would she say? It was too late to say anything. If only she'd checked her messages sooner.

She had sat in Matt's apartment, hiding out like no one else in the world mattered, and now her self-indulgence had cost the most respected man she knew, his company.

Robert pulled up to the apartment building and ran out to open her door before she could object. "If you don't let me do my job, people might start to question my job performance," he said, looking at Jerry, who was walking toward the front doors.

"Thank you," said Trudy. "You're right. I've caused enough trouble for today."

She got out of the car and strode past Jerry. "Good day, Ms. Allen," he said, holding the doors open.

Trudy simply nodded and continued to the elevators.

Matt was standing in the hallway when she stepped off the elevator. "Trudy, thank God, you're okay. Robert just called to let me know he found you."

Trudy went into the apartment, saying nothing.

"Trudy." Matt placed his hand on her shoulder. "We need to talk."

Trudy stopped and turned to stare down at his hand. Her whole body vibrated with animosity. "Please get your hands off of me," she spat.

Matt snatched his hand back. "Sorry, but we need to talk. I know you probably hate me right now but let me explain."

"What is there to explain?" Trudy rotated, facing him. "How you pursued me with the intention of getting me out of the way to steal my boss's company? How you made me look like a fool? How you made me trust you? Is that what you want to talk about? How Mr. Dalsin wouldn't sell you his company, so it made more sense to steal it out from under him?"

"There is so much opportunity in that little hardware store, and Mr. Dalsin is doing nothing…nothing to take advantage of it," Matt exclaimed. "There is so much potential there."

Trudy regarded Matt as if he were mad. "And for some reason, you think that it's your right to take something that someone else spent years building, steal it from them, and use it to your advantage? But why not, right? I suppose to you in some twisted way it makes sense," she sighed. "Because you had no problem when it came to interfering in my marriage to get what you wanted."

Trudy waited a moment to let Matt respond, but when he said nothing, she headed to her room. He followed.

She went to her closet, pulled out her suitcase, and laid it on the bed.

"What are you doing?" Matt asked.

“Packing.”

“I know that, but why? You don’t have to leave.” He reached his hand out to stop her, but seemed to think better of it.

“You got what you wanted. I played my part.”

“I meant what I said. Everything we talked about this past weekend. About you staying and the kids coming here to visit.”

“You’re joking, right?” Trudy shot Matt a look before turning to empty the dresser drawers, making sure to leave behind the clothes that Matt had bought her.

“I know things between us didn’t start off on the right foot—”

“You think?” Trudy snapped.

“But,” Matt started again. “Since you’ve been here, I’ve grown to care for you. I mean, I did try and push you away at first, but that was because of the circumstances behind me bringing you here in the first place. In the beginning, it didn’t feel right, knowing that…but now that *you* know,” he said, meeting her eyes. “Now that everything is out in the open, things can be different. I think over time, it could become something stronger. Maybe even love.”

Trudy felt a sharp pain in her chest. Love. He had toyed with her feelings for over a month, convincing her to run away and move in with him, only to start treating her like a stranger once she got here. The whole time, she had questioned his sudden change but still prayed he would eventually begin to show her some sort of affection. Enough to let her know that leaving her family had been for…something. And now, after she found out he had betrayed her, he wanted to talk about love.

“Do you actually think that I could stay here knowing

everything I know now? I turned my back on my family, my son. I am responsible for Mr. Dalsin losing his company." Trudy regarded Matt with a hopeful expression. "Unless you've changed your mind?"

Matt shook his head. "There are other investors. It's too late."

Trudy exhaled. "Do you think I could live here and face myself each day knowing my part in this? Do you even know me? I guess not," she sighed. "That was never the point of all this anyways, was it?"

"No," Matt confessed. "But I want to know you now."

Trudy hung her head. "Matt. I am not going to stay here. I can't. I won't."

"Okay, but at least stay until the morning. You can catch a flight out then. I'll pay for it."

"I don't want anything from you."

"Trudy, I know you're mad, but you don't get paid until tomorrow. Let me do this last thing for you. It's the least I can do."

"Whatever," said Trudy. "Do whatever. The sooner, the better. Can you leave me alone now?"

She watched as Matt walked out of the room and closed the door behind him. For the first time since Trudy met him, he appeared defeated.

Trudy finished packing her suitcase, zipped it closed, and placed it back on the floor. She climbed into the bed and pulled her knees to her. A few seconds later, tears began flowing ferociously down her face. An hour later, she was asleep.

CHAPTER 13

T HE PLANE TOUCHED down over an hour ago, and
Trudy was now in a Lyft on her way home. She'd left
Texas at ten o'clock this morning, but with the time
change and a four-hour flight, it was now seven o'clock at
night.

Trudy texted James before getting on the plane to let him
know she was coming home, but he had not responded back.

The Lyft pulled up outside the house. Most of the lights
were still on. Both her and James's cars were in the driveway.
Trudy paid the driver through the app on her phone and got
out, pulling her suitcase behind her.

A face peeked out from the blinds of Cori's bedroom
window. The sound of the car pulling up must have alerted
them to her arrival.

On the way up the walk, Trudy searched in her purse for
her house keys. Eventually, her hand landed on metal, and
she pulled out the keyring, searching until she found the two
keys for the top and bottom locks.

She placed her key into the doorknob and turned, but
nothing happened. She tried the top lock; her key would not
work there either. She was about to ring the doorbell when

the door opened in front of her.

"Can I help you?" asked James, both eyebrows arched high above his forehead.

Trudy wondered how long he had been listening to her failed attempts from inside the house. "I'm trying to come in."

"Sorry, but, that's not going to happen."

"What do you mean?" Trudy stared at him incredulously. "The last time we talked, you asked me to come home."

"And that was days ago. When I didn't hear from you, I retained a lawyer and filed for divorce and abandonment."

Trudy gawked at him. "You did what?"

"You heard me."

Through a crack in the door, Trudy could see Eric standing off to the side, holding a game controller in his hand. "Hi, baby," she called out to him.

"Hey, mom. I missed you." Eric said.

"I missed you too. Where's your sister?" Trudy raised her voice, hoping it would carry upstairs to where she knew Cori was listening.

James moved over, blocking Trudy's view of Eric. "Evidently, you didn't miss your kids *too* much, seeing how you abandoned your family in the middle of the night."

"I know that. Okay?" Trudy met James's eyes, searching. "But I'm here now."

"It's too late."

"James, I know you're angry, but we can work this out." Trudy pleaded.

"What is there to work out?" he asked. "Are you saying that you came back because you realized you still love me?Or did you come back because of what happened to Mr. Dalsin?"

"How did you know about that?" asked Trudy, caught off guard.

"Mr. Dalsin called me when he could not get in touch with you."

There was no point in pretending that she could simply show up and reconcile with her family as if nothing significant had transpired. James knew the truth, and Trudy wasn't even sure what she expected when she had come back anyway. James and both the kids welcoming her with open arms? She and James sharing a bed again as if nothing had happened?

"Can I at least see the kids?"

"You've seen Eric, and Cori has nothing to say to you."

Trudy stepped back, gazed up at Cori's window, and saw that there was still a gap in the blinds. It closed as soon as Cori realized she had been caught watching.

"James," Trudy said, turning back to him. "I'm sorry that things turned out this way. I never intended…" Trudy trailed off, unable to finish the sentence.

James met her eyes. The look he gave her said, that either he didn't believe she was sorry, or he didn't care. Trudy could not be sure. She wasn't able to read him as she once could. He had changed so much over the last couple of weeks. He was now harder and even more guarded than before. "We'll try to work something out with custody. I know Eric still wants to see you."

Trudy nodded. "I guess it's okay if I take my car?"

"I don't see why not," James answered, unconcerned.

"I love you, Eric," Trudy yelled inside the house. "You too, Cori," she called out to the window upstairs.

Trudy went to her car, opened the back seat, and placed her suitcase inside. She climbed into the driver's seat and slowly backed out of the driveway, hoping James would change his mind. But all she saw was the front door closing.

❧

Trudy was lying on top of the bed in her hotel room with chips, snack cakes, and sodas spread out in front of her. She had purchased the rations from a nearby convenience store, while feeling sorry for herself.

She picked up the remote and began flipping through the TV for something to watch. Over a hundred channels and there was nothing on—nothing except for the news and an old black-and-white movie, *The Shop Around the Corner*. She and Matt had watched it in bed together this past weekend. In the end, the two love interests, who have been fighting throughout the entire movie, realize they have already fallen in love through their correspondence as pen pals. The film closes with the two lovers staring dreamingly into each other's eyes.

Trudy turned off the TV and shoved a snack cake in her mouth.

Regardless of Matt's part in all of this, she knew that her current situation was of her own making. Shawna would have said she was a grown woman, making grown women's decisions. Trudy had not been happy in her life, and Matt had been more than willing to use it to his advantage.

She had seen the shiny object twinkling beneath the sewer grate and, after taking the time to fish it out, found it to be nothing more than a discarded silver gum wrapper.

Now with James filing for divorce and citing Trudy with abandonment, she would need a job and a lawyer of her own. Trudy wondered where James had gotten the funds to secure an attorney. She still had access to all the accounts, and none

240

of the money had been touched, other than to pay a few household bills. No doubt, James's family already had a business lawyer on retainer. *That* they had money for.

Trudy checked the account she'd opened when she first started working for Kelly Enterprises, once she found herself in need of a hotel room for the night. The account had shown a deposit of $25,000 along with her pay for the week. The $25,000 must have been Matt's attempt at an apology. Trudy considered sending the money back, but she knew she would need it.

In the morning, Trudy would have to start looking for a place to live, a job, and retain her own Family Law attorney. But first, she would need to visit Mr. Dalsin. It was time she began to face up to her mistakes.

Trudy pulled into the hardware store's parking lot. Although the lot was unusually full for this time of day, she was able to find a space. The first thing she noticed was the 'Going Out of Business' sign in the store's front window.

Inside, most of the shelves were empty. The line at the register made its way down one aisle and wrapped around another. Trudy nodded at Jennifer as she squeezed between two customers.

On her way to see Mr. Dalsin, Trudy passed her old office. She glanced inside and saw that all the furniture, except for her chair, was gone. Most likely sold off as part of the store closing.

Mr. Dalsin was in his office with Peggy when Trudy knocked on the door.

Peggy looked up. "Hi," she smiled. "I'm going to leave the two of you alone." Peggy picked up the ledgers they had been going over, taking them with her.

"I see you're pretty busy," said Trudy, nodding her head toward the front of the store. "I won't stay long. I was just coming by to check in and see how things were going."

"Yes, we are swamped. I'd offer you a job, but…" Mr. Dalsin trailed off, his attempt at a joke falling flat.

"I am sorry for everything. Had I known—"

Mr. Dalsin held his hand up, waving her off. "It's not your fault. This is not your doing. I should have been on the lookout when Matt first tried to buy my business. It's my fault for not doing my due diligence. I'm too trusting. Maybe it's for the best. The world, as I knew it, no longer exists. People are becoming ruthless, and all they seem to care about is money. The customer no longer matters." Mr. Dalsin's eyes glazed over as he stared off into the corner of his office, as if picturing a time when things were simpler.

Trudy, too, longed for a simpler time. For her, that would have been over a month ago, before Matt reentered her life, when she worked at the hardware store, and she still had Shawna to call on when she needed someone to talk to. Trudy wished she could be as forgiving as Mr. Dalsin and accept the hand that she'd been dealt.

"I think I'm going to go now," Trudy said, interrupting Mr. Dalsin's stupor.

"You may want to stop by and see Peggy first. She has a few of your things in her office. But before you leave," Mr. Dalsin walked from behind his desk, holding his arms out in front of him. "A hug. I don't know when I'll see you again."

Trudy allowed Mr. Dalsin to embrace her as she hugged him back.

"It's going to be alright," he said, patting her on the back. "Things will work themselves out. Unfortunately, we must all venture through dark times in our lives. They are there to teach us lessons, and when we come out on the other side, we're a little better for it."

"I hope so," said Trudy, pulling away. "I wish I had a fraction of your strength."

"Well, I've lived a little longer than you," Mr. Dalsin gave her a wink before going back to his desk and sitting down. "But…I'm sure you'd be surprised at how strong you actually are."

Trudy wasn't sure about that. If she appeared strong, it was a façade —a mask she showed the outside world while she was slowly unraveling on the inside.

"I'm going to let you get back to your day," she said, giving him a half-smile.

"Thank you for stopping by, Trudy. Don't be a stranger. I'm not sure what will become of this place," Mr. Dalsin said, sweeping his hand around the room. "But you and your family are always welcome in my home. And be sure to let Peggy know if you need a job reference."

"Thank you. Mr. Dalsin. After all that's happened, that means the world to me." Trudy said, her eyes filling up with tears.

"I told you, Trudy. I don't blame you. We probably wouldn't have come this far without you."

Trudy simply nodded and took her leave.

Peggy, who had been standing in the hallway, handed her a Bankers box with her things inside. Trudy took the box and smiled at her through the tears streaming down her face. Peggy patted her on the shoulder but said nothing.

Trudy made her way through the customers standing in line, and walked out of Dalsin's and Son for the last time.

Trudy spent the rest of the day sending resumés to

employers. Most of the requirements for the positions she'd found, were for only half the work she'd done at the hardware store. And the pay, was less than the salary she'd earned while working there.

It was starting to look as though Trudy was going to need two jobs to maintain a lifestyle on her own and any child support she would be required to pay to James.

There were a few two-bedroom apartments near the house that she would be viewing after meeting with an attorney tomorrow. Hopefully, James would allow Eric to come and visit. She would have to get Eric his own bedroom set even if she had to sleep on the floor.

"Hope you're doing well today. You can have a seat while I look over your information." Lucy McKenny of Fulton McKenny and Owens stared at the monitor on her desk, reviewing the material Trudy submitted a few days ago.

The leather plush chair chosen for comfort, might as well have been made of stone. Trudy could not sit still and kept fidgeting with her purse.

Lucy looked up to face Trudy and locked her fingers in front of her, on top of the mahogany-stained desk. Lucy's thick black hair was styled into a bob that framed her face. She was a handsome woman with sculpted features. The expression she wore was stern and forthright. "Do you know who your husband's attorney is?"

"No, I have no idea," answered Trudy, shaking her head.

Lucy picked up a pen and began making notes on a yellow pad. "I'll need to find out. You said you were staying in a hotel right now. Is that correct?"

"Yes."

"Have you made your whereabouts known to your husband so, he has an address to serve you any legal documents?"

"I've texted him the information, but he hasn't responded."

"Good. Text messages show a record. Make sure you keep any messages between you and… James. Right?

Trudy nodded.

"You and James in the coming weeks. As a matter of fact," Lucy looked up from her notes. "Can you take a screenshot and forward me the text messages?"

"Sure," answered Trudy.

"And you do plan on moving from the hotel and finding some sort of stable residence, soon?"

"Yes," said Trudy. Although this was a simple consultation, she felt as if she were sitting on the stand being interrogated.

Lucy laid her pen down and pursed her lips together as she entwined her fingers once again. "I can tell you right now, things don't look that good for you, unless…you can prove some sort of discretion on James's part. Was there any type of mental or physical abuse in your marriage?"

"No," Trudy answered.

"Any infidelity on his part?"

"No." Trudy shook her head.

"Are you sure? Not even a hint of indiscretion over the years?"

"James went to work and came home. Once he started working third shift, if he had any free time, it was spent in bed. But he does work for his family, and they rarely pay him. Which ended up leaving me as the main supporter of the household." Trudy added, hopeful.

Lucy slowly shook her head. "Unfortunately, that helps his case more than yours. The fact that he earned less than half of your yearly income gives him a case for alimony. Based on the numbers you gave me, you are looking at about fifteen hundred a month in alimony and eight hundred in child support."

"But I'm not even working right now." Trudy scoffed.

"But you are able to. My suggestion is to find a job soon. I think that is all for today." Lucy pushed away from her desk. "You and I most likely will not meet again until you've been served by James's lawyer. If I need any additional information, I will email you. I'll also be sending you a bill for today's session." Lucy stood up and extended her hand to Trudy. "Enjoy the rest of your day."

Easier said than done.

Trudy shook hands with Lucy and left.

The first thing Trudy noticed was the For Sale sign in the front yard. She pulled into the driveway, parked her car, and got out. Walking up to one of the front windows, she cupped her hands and peered inside. The house was empty.

She had tried calling Shawna's phone again for what seemed like the hundredth time. Before, the phone would ring and eventually go to voicemail, but this time, Trudy had gotten a message that the number was no longer in service.

She sat down on one of the steps of the small portico leading to the front door.

Where had they gone?

Like her, Shawna was no longer close with any of her family. And as far as Trudy knew, Greg's parents were dead, and he had no other siblings. Surely, Greg had not decided to pack up and move just to get away from *her*. And why had Shawna not tried to reach out to Trudy before leaving?

Placing her elbows on her knees, Trudy settled her chin into her palms and took a deep breath. She had hoped that things would have gotten better since her last update on Shawna before leaving town. Trudy had assumed that once Greg calmed down, he would have stopped blaming her for the problems in his marriage. That maybe he and Shawna would have sought counseling, and eventually, she and Shawna could have begun communicating again, even if it had only been through phone calls.

But now, with their moving away and Shawna's phone turned off, any hope of that was lost, at least for the time being.

Trudy got up from the stoop and went back to her car. Maybe there was a way for her to track Shawna down. It was worth a shot. People didn't just disappear into thin air. She just hoped that with whatever was going on, that Shawna was okay. Even if she never spoke to her again, Trudy prayed that wherever she was, she was happy.

CHAPTER 14

"HI," TRUDY PURSED her lips together in a half-hearted attempt at a smile. "Is Eric ready?" she asked James.

It had been six months since the divorce, but things between her and James were still awkward. Although she knew the end of her marriage had ultimately been her fault—at least, that was how it was stated on the divorce decree. Well, technically the state listed it as a no-fault divorce, but it was still left to the discretion of the judge, who had shown immense dislike toward Trudy—she felt as if she had been given the short end of the stick.

It had not helped Trudy's case that she had left her family in the middle of the night, without any notice, to be with another man. The judge had not looked too kindly on her for her actions and granted James everything he and his lawyer had asked for, which included the house, alimony, and child support.

Knowing that over a third of her income was going to James until Eric was of age and James remarried, made it hard for Trudy to remain civil towards him whenever she came to pick up their son. It had been bad enough that they had struggled financially during their marriage because of him, but now he was being rewarded for it.

"He'll be out soon. I think he's trying to get his gaming system together. You know, it might be easier if he had a system here and one at your apartment as well."

Trudy gave James a half-hearted smile. No doubt she would be the one purchasing said system. "Were you planning on chipping in?" Trudy asked.

James opened his mouth to respond just as Eric came out of the house. He ran past his dad to give Trudy a hug, nearly knocking her down. "Woah there," said Trudy. "You're getting kind of big."

"Where's my hug?" James asked.

Eric gave his dad a strange look but turned back and hugged him.

When did he get so paternal?

Trudy was surprised James was even out of bed at this time of day. She wondered if his hours had changed but knew she was no longer in a place that allowed her to ask those types of questions.

"Let's get this weekend started." Trudy headed to the car to put Eric's things in the back seat. While she was placing his backpack and duffle bag inside, she heard a voice call out to her.

"Hey, Mom." Cori had come out of the house and was now standing beside her father.

Cori was home for spring break. A few months ago, she had unblocked Trudy's number, and they were now texting each other a few times a week. Her messages mostly consisted of how she was getting along in her classes and sometimes asking for help with Math.

With Cori away at college, and even though she agreed to

texting, Cori had still refused to see Trudy, so other than the photos she received from Eric, this was the first time Trudy had seen her daughter in about a year.

Although she was only eighteen, Cori seemed much older and more mature than the last time Trudy had seen her. It took everything in her not to run back towards the house and give her daughter a hug. But she knew that would be a big mistake. If she pushed too hard, that would just send her daughter running in the opposite direction. She'd follow Cori's lead and move at the pace that she set for their relationship.

Even though they were barely speaking, their interactions were no longer volatile as they had been before Trudy left last spring. Hopefully, within a few years, it would mirror some semblance of the perfect mother-daughter relationship that Trudy had always hoped for.

"You guys, take care," Trudy called out of the window as she backed out of the driveway. "So, what do you want to do this weekend?" she asked, turning to Eric.

"I was thinking we could play Scribblenauts."

Trudy cringed. "Eric, you know I hate that game. I have no idea what I'm doing. At least with the fighting games, I can smash random buttons and hopefully end up with the right combination and do some damage."

Eric sat for a minute, contemplating as he tapped his finger against his chin. "Maybe the arcade. That way, we can walk through the mall afterward and get a pretzel."

"Sounds like a plan," Trudy said, smiling.

Even with the weeks flying by, now that she commuted out of town for work, having Eric with her every other weekend never felt like enough. After struggling to pay alimony, child support, and maintain her own bills, Trudy had reached out to Beverly to see if the job she had offered her was still available; fortunately, it had.

On their way to the arcade, Trudy passed by what used to be Dalsin's and Son. Although Matt and his investors had been able to buy the land and raise the rent, they had not been able to persuade Mr. Dalsin to sell his store to them.

After the store closed, the original building was torn down and replaced by one twice its size. The new building was fashioned along the lines of the mass warehouse-style home improvement stores. Trudy had driven by a few times but had never been inside.

Despite the store being busy during the first week of its grand opening, the parking lot now barely held any cars. The financial reports that Trudy read predicted that if revenue did not pick up soon, the store would be closing in less than a year.

It appeared that without the name Dalsin's and Son and Matt's refusal to incorporate the same system that Mr. Dalsin used to run his store, that all his efforts had been for naught. Kelly Enterprises' grand idea of turning Dalsin's and Son into another mass retail store, as was listed in the company's financial projections, had failed.

After closing Dalsin's & Son, Mr. Dalsin did end up retiring. However, it was not before he purchased land of his own a few miles from the original location. A new hardware store, solely called Dalsin's, had been erected and was now being run by his son John.

Mr. Dalsin had offered Trudy her old job back, but she had turned him down. As much as she had loved working for Mr. Dalsin and had come to terms with the fact that she was not responsible for Matt's actions, it was time for her to move on with the next chapter of her life. Besides, with Mr.

Dalsin's desire to remain a small Mom and Pop store, the salary for her position would never have been enough.

Although it meant the world to her, to be able to spend time out with her son, Trudy was glad to be back at her apartment. She and Eric had killed a few zombies, been tossed around virtually, and lasered very successfully by two other boys, before heading to the food court for not only pretzels, but pizza and frozen yogurt as well.

Trudy did not know how it was possible for one boy to eat so much or where he was even putting it. Eric still sported a lean build, and was growing at what appeared to be, by the second. He was nearly six feet tall, and it felt awkward whenever Trudy had to look up when responding to her teenage son.

Trudy was sitting on the sofa with her feet propped up as she sorted through her mail, while she and Eric waited for a game to finish updating on his game system.

"Mom, did you get the cheese puffs I like?" asked Eric from inside the kitchen.

"Cheese puffs?" Trudy called out. "Are you eating *again*?"

"Like you're always saying, I'm a growing boy."

"Please tell me you're finished. You keep growing, I'm going to need a bigger apartment." Trudy teased. "I think they're on top of the refrigerator."

Trudy was just about to toss the stack of bills and junk mail, when the last envelope caught her eye. It was a simple white envelope addressed to her, with no other information. However, Trudy recognized the handwriting immediately.

"What's this?" she mumbled aloud.

"Everything okay?" asked Eric, coming out of the kitchen, his mouth full of cheese puffs.

"I think Shawna wrote me a letter," Trudy said, sliding her finger through the seal of the envelope.

Inside was a single sheet of paper. Seeing her name scrawled at the top in Shawna's penscript, Trudy felt the sting of tears in her eyes.

Trudy,

> *I know it seems that I dropped off the face of the Earth, but I want you to know that I am okay and still thinking of you. I want you to know that I appreciate you always being there for me and everything you've done. Even though I know that I was not always the best friend, I could have been for you. I know there were times where the things I said were harsh, and it may have felt as if I was trying to tear you down, but that was never my intentions. As a friend, I should have always been the one to build you up. It should never have been said that I could be the one that caused you pain, because I love and support you in everything that you do, as you have always done for me. And I'm sorry that I was not always there to wish you well. I just think that I was projecting onto you how I felt about myself. I had no right to meddle in your family business when things were not right in my own home.*

> *Again, I'm Sorry. I just needed you to know this, and I hope somehow, you've always known how I really feel.*

Trudy placed the letter back into the envelope and laid it on the coffee table before wiping her eyes. Although she had come to a place in her life where she was content, the constant worry over her friend's whereabouts and how she was doing had weighed on her heavily over the last year. She was happy to finally have some closure.

"Are those happy tears or sad tears?" asked Eric.

"A little bit of both," Trudy said, giving him a small smile.

"Still want to play me in Mario Kart, or are you too sad right now?"

Trudy looked at the TV screen and saw that the game was waiting for her to choose her character.

"Not only can I play, get ready to be annihilated." Trudy grabbed her controller off the TV stand.

"Mom," said Eric, rolling his eyes. "It's not that type of game."

"You say that now, but wait until you're slipping all over one of my banana peels."

"Whatever," Eric taunted. "You can barely keep your car on the track."

Trudy selected her character and her car and leaned back against the couch with her legs folded under her, preparing herself to be beaten unmercifully by her son in one of his favorite video games. To her, it didn't matter if she ever learned the ins and outs of the game; she was just happy that Eric wanted to play with her even though they both knew she would never be any sort of competition.

When the game began, Trudy watched as every car shot passed the starting line except hers. For some reason, her car remained stagnant and refused to pick up speed. "Hey, what's going on? My car won't move?"

"Sorry, Mom. Can't help you right now. Maybe you can toss out one of those banana peels and see if it will help you." Eric said joking.

Trudy picked one of the pillows off the couch and threw it at him. "Smart Alec."

She watched as he deftly swatted the pillow away and continued maneuvering his car around the track, swiftly avoiding obstacles, and picking up shells, mushrooms, and coins along the way.

If it were not for the fact that she knew she would upset him by ruining his game, she would grab Eric in her arms and plant wet kisses all over his face. Trudy knew that she had been lucky that he had been so willing to forgive her. As she stared at him, she swore she would do everything she could within her power to never cause him harm again.

"You can't win the game if you're staring at me," Eric noted.

"I can't help it if I like looking at my handsome son."

"Whatever," Eric said, casting her a look of exasperation. "Eyes on the road."

"Yes sir," said Trudy, knowing that any hopes of her even placing were a lost cause.

She turned to the TV and somehow managed to find the correct button to get her car moving through the course. As she watched her car fall in line behind the others, she thought of how much the game mirrored her life. It had taken a while for her to get moving after returning home from Texas, and in the beginning, it had felt like adversaries were constantly tossing things at her to trip her up, but now it felt as if all of that were in her past, and somehow and some way she would eventually make it to the finish line. Whether it was in first place or last, she would accept it as a victory, and be patient with any obstacles that life chose to place in front of her, because she knew that she was doing everything she could, to make it there.

READ ON
FOR AN EXCERPT
OF T. ATKINS'
NEWEST NOVEL

Beneath the Surface of Content

I COUNT THE BEAMS of sunlight flowing through the cracks in the blinds as they stream across the bedroom wall. The simple exertion causes my swollen eye to tear up.

I cautiously place my fingers against my left eyelid and feel the spongy flesh, making me wince. I have not yet found the courage to check my eye in the mirror, but I know it will be several days, if not a week, before it appears anything close to normal again.

Although it had felt good to lash out at the time, spewing out the callous words and seeing the wounded expression on Greg's face—even if it had only lasted for a second—I now regretted my decision. Greg's hurt had quickly turned to rage, and I silently watched as his hand closed into a fist, swung out, and made contact with my eye.

Despite the fact that our argument had started over his photos. The instant photos I'd found tucked away in the back of his drawer—pictures of him and women performing sexual acts on each other. Somehow, I had become the villain.

He had come into the room and found me sitting on the bed, looking through them. Instead of showing any sort of shame, Greg had immediately turned on me, wanting to know why I had been going through his things. After going back and forth and yelling about which one of us was in the wrong, I realized I was not going to get any real answers out of him. I suddenly felt the need to make him feel at least an ounce of my pain and betrayal.

I yelled out. "Fine. You know what, Greg? I don't care what you do. Do what you want. It's not like I'm not fucking somebody too!"

A hushed silence fell over the room before a look of hurt and understanding had appeared across his face. "What do you mean…somebody else?" Greg had ground out between his teeth.

"You heard me. I've been fucking someone else, too," I spewed out again in the heat of anger. And although it had not been true, somehow, that little lie had made me the culprit. Never mind the fact that the evidence of his deeds were spread across our marriage bed.

And, of course, it had only made sense for Greg to blame my best friend Trudy for instigating the whole thing.

"I know that friend of yours put you up to this." Greg spat out the word friend like it left a bad taste in his mouth. He paced back and forth, cradling his hand as I lay sprawled across the bed, with my hand shielding my eye as I sobbed into the bed sheets.

"I knew it wasn't a good idea to move back here after getting out." He stopped pacing and turned sharply, facing the bed. "I better not catch you talking to her again. You hear me, Shawna?! You hear me?!" he yelled again before charging out of the bedroom.

I laid on the bed listening for what felt like an eternity before I heard the front door close, and Greg's car peeling out of the driveway a few seconds later. I had lain there for another thirty minutes crying and feeling sorry for myself before remembering that Shawna Jane Hall was better than this. Even if I had allowed myself to become a doormat, I was nobody's punching bag.

Sure, I had allowed Greg to manipulate me into being what he thought was the perfect wife. If the word 'wife' were an object. Over the years, I had grown to feel more like a thing than a person. I had allowed him to control every aspect of my life, including who I talked to and spent time with and even what I wore.

Funny thing was, it hadn't always been this way. When Greg and I first met in high school, he had been more easygoing, but once he joined the military and we were stationed overseas, where I had no one but him to rely on, and barely understood the language, he'd changed.

But through all the manipulations and berating me when he deemed I had fallen out of line, he had never hit me. There had been the bruises on my arms from the times when he had grabbed or shoved me, where I'd ended up landing against a table or countertop, but this was the first time he had left a mark that a simple pullover could not cover up.

I had been in a few fights growing up and some in high school. Most had been between boys who had been running their mouths about me or Trudy, laughing at our second-hand clothes. But growing up with my male cousins had taught me quickly how to take care of myself, and soon, not even the girls at school thought about challenging me.

Now, I barely recognized the woman I had become. Lying here like some empty shell. Some pathetic version of a woman that I would have made fun of in my past life.

It's eight o'clock in the morning, and Greg has not made it home. I wonder which of the women in the pictures he chose to spend the night with.

I get up from the bed and make my way to the bathroom to stare at myself in the mirror. There's no way I'm going to be meeting Trudy today, even if Greg hadn't forbidden me to do so. I'll have to find my phone and message her that I won't be coming.

I already know she's going to be upset. Since moving back to town, our time together has become more and more less frequent. I can tell that Trudy's independent nature and ease of showing up whenever she wants to, makes Greg uncomfortable even if he won't admit it.

A few times after Greg found out that Trudy was the main provider of her household, he had made snide comments under his breath. He had grown up with beliefs of what a man and woman's place in the household was. And Trudy was not it.

Greg has refused to let me work. Not even from home. In the beginning, I thought it was sweet, but I've grown to realize it was just another form of manipulation and a way for him to keep tabs on me. And any time I've ever gotten close to any woman in the past, he's figured out a way to end the relationship. I'm surprised that he had allowed Trudy and I to be close for so long, but I knew that in time, it would end.

Even before blaming Trudy for my fake cheating, he had already begun to imply that he didn't trust her. Leaving the house one day, he had passed her on her way coming to see me. When he returned that evening, he said something about the way Trudy looked at him that day, made him think she was sneaky. And he did not like sneaky people.

But I suppose, that would mean he doesn't care much for himself, considering all the pictures I found hidden away in the back of his drawer. If you don't call that sneaky, I don't know what is. And Greg had been at this for a while. He had to have been… to have left those pictures in his dresser drawer, meant he had become complacent and wasn't worried about me finding them.

I walk back into the bedroom, pick up my phone from the nightstand. Before I call Trudy, I need to make sure none of the anger or resentment I am currently feeling comes through. I have been able to keep the current circumstances of my marriage from her, and I don't need her realizing something is wrong and rushing over here. I could never face her looking like this.

I take a deep breath, count to ten, then dial her number. She picks up on the second ring.

"Shawna, I was just about to call you."

"Ah, how sweet. Glad to know, I'm the first thing you think of every morning."

"I was going to make sure we were still on for today," she says, ignoring my small attempt at humor.

"About that…"

"Shawna. Seriously." Trudy's voice rises, irritated. "You know what, I'm sorry. Is everything okay?"

Okay, that's more like it. Trudy has always been slow to anger and doesn't like stirring things up. Although, sometimes, I wish she would. As much as I try to keep what's going on at home away from her, I wish she would ask more questions and try to find out why I've begun to grow more distant. Sometimes, I wish she would call me out on my bullshit. But it's not her role in our relationship. It's mine.

"Girl, yes. I'm sorry I'm going to have to cancel, again. It's just, I woke up this morning a little nauseous. Feels like a migraine coming on."

I lie. I've never had a migraine in my life.

"I didn't realize you suffered from…" she trails off. "You said you were nauseous. You don't think you might be…?"

I pull the phone away, cover it with my hand, and choke back a laugh. Unless Greg had his vasectomy reversed without telling me. Besides, he hadn't touched me in over a month.

"No, no," I say, putting the phone back to my ear. "I'm sure that's not it."

There's silence on her end. Not sure what she's thinking.

"But anyway. I think it would be best for me to rest now."

"Yeah, I understand. Feel better, okay?" Trudy says.

"I will. Thanks." I smile, knowing she is worried about me.

I'm just about to end the call when she says. "Shawna. You know I'm here if you need me?"

"Girl, yeah. I know," I say, trying to make light of the situation. "But nothing a couple of Excedrin won't fix."

I poke my swollen eyelid with my finger. If only.